My Fat Dog

Ten Simple Steps to Help Your Pet
Lose Weight for a Long and Happy Life

My Fat Dog

Ten Simple Steps to Help Your Pet
Lose Weight for a Long and Happy Life

Martha Garvey

**Foreword by Deborah Greco, D.V.M., Ph.D.,
The Animal Medical Center**

Illustrations by Sebastian Conley

healthyliving**books**

New York · London

A Healthy Living Book
Published by Hatherleigh Press
5-22 46th Avenue, Suite 200
Long Island City, NY 11101
www.hatherleighpress.com

Library of Congress Cataloging-in-Publication Data

Garvey, Martha.
   My fat dog : ten simple steps to help your pet lose weight for a long and
happy life / Martha Garvey ; foreword by Deborah Greco.
      p. cm.
   Includes bibliographical references and index.
   ISBN 1-57826-198-8 (alk. paper)
   1. Dogs—Diseases—Diet therapy. 2. Dogs—Exercise. 3. Dogs—Health. 4.
Obesity in animals. I. Title.
   SF991.G38 2005
   636.7'0895854--dc22
                                   2005012409

Disclaimer
The information in this book is meant to be used under the supervision of a veterinarian, and you should get approval before beginning a regimen. The author, editors, and publisher disclaim any liability or loss in connection with the use of this book or advice within.

All Healthy Living Books are available for bulk purchase, special promotions, and premiums. For information on reselling and special purchase opportunities, call 1-800-528-2550 and ask for the Special Sales Manager.

Interior design by Deborah Miller, Phillip Mondestin, Jacinta Monniere
Cover design by Deborah Miller & Phillip Mondestin

10 9 8 7 6 5 4 3 2 1
Printed in Canada

For Jeff and Faith

In memory of Odie, Mr. Pleasure Dog

Contents

Acknowledgments

No book ever gets written without the help of lots of fantastic people (and in this book's case, a few great dogs). Thanks to everyone who told me their stories, shared pictures, provided diet and training tips, and just plain loved their dogs. Thank you to: Amy Rea, Bill Bishop, Cathy Sutherland, David Muriello, Dr. Andrew Kaplan, Dr. Bob Goldstein, Dr. Jennifer Jellison, Dr. Martha Gearhart, Dr. Phil Brown, Janine Adams, Jennifer Teitler, Jon Katz, Joyce Darrell, Kathleen Reilly, Liz Lane, Mark Robinson, Pamela Dennison, Raluca State, Renee DeLuca, Stephen Payne, Terry Miller Shannon, Penny Wagner, the staffs at the Liberty Humane Shelter, the Assisi Center, Beowoof, Animal Pantry, Hoboken Animal Hospital, the Dog Run, the Hoboken Public Library, and my online companions at Freelance Success, Readerville, and the Utne Café.

Extra special thanks to Stephany Evans, intrepid agent, and Andrea Au, sharp-eyed editor. They are a writer's best friends.

Foreword

It is estimated that more than 100 million Americans are overweight and that 25 to 45 percent of our pets are overweight. Recent books and films, such as *Fast Food Nation* and *Super Size Me,* have laid bare both the causes and the consequences for people of our current culture of too little exercise and too much snacking. But what about our best friends?

Obesity in dogs may be a consequence of overeating rooted in pack behavior; dogs eat as much as they can when food is abundant because they do not know when the next meal is coming. However, more often dog owners are simply unaware of the amount of calories in dog snacks and overfeed out of ignorance. An average sized 40-pound dog should be eating about 1200 kcal per day, or about 3 cups of dry food. The owner puts the food down twice daily and the dog eats it.

But the dog probably also gets three treats per day with an average calorie count of 200 kcal/treat. If the owner is feeding a "rounded" cup as opposed to a "level" cup of food, the extra kibble in the rounded cup will amount to approximately 3 cups of food in a week (600 excess calories/week). If the dog is walked only once a day and is discouraged from playing too vigorously in the house, those calories will soon translate to extra pounds. Once owners understand the math behind overfeeding, they can prevent obesity in their dogs by simply feeding them fewer treats and walking them more often.

Simple, however, isn't always easy, and that's where *My Fat Dog* comes in. *My Fat Dog* outlines a creative approach to helping dogs stay slim and healthy, exploring the roots of canine obesity and explaining why our dogs are fat. As a veterinarian who is frustrated by seeing so many dogs with obesity-related disorders, such as arthritis, I was particularly interested in Ms. Garvey's suggestions and practical tips for instituting a weight-loss program in dogs. From creating a "dog log" to track your pet's progress to adding a few vegetables to his diet to playing hide-and-seek to force him to earn his treats, this book gives you easy and effective tools that you can start doing immediately to help your dog get—and stay—trim and healthy.

Recent data shows that if you keep your dog lean, you may be able to extend his or her life by as much as two years. And as everyone knows, a dog's life is too short as it is. I would be willing to do anything in order to have two more years with my beloved Standard poodle, Martini. I think I'll start by reducing his food intake and increasing his exercise. Then I'll go fetch a copy of this book.

—Deborah Greco, D.V.M., Ph.D.

Deborah Greco, D.V.M., Ph.D., is currently a staff endocrinologist at The Animal Medical Center in New York. The recipient of the Pfizer award for research excellence and the American Association of Feline Practitioners research award for her work on feline diabetes mellitus, Dr. Greco was a professor of small animal internal medicine at Colorado State University for twelve years. A diplomate of the American College of Veterinary Internal Medicine, she received her D.V.M. from the University of California and her Ph.D. from Texas A&M University.

Find Out If Your Dog Is Really Fat

It doesn't happen overnight. You're playing catch with your mighty retriever, and you notice that not only is he not retrieving like he used to, his sleek silhouette is more Hardy than Laurel, more John Goodman than Brad Pitt. He's walking when he used to gallop. He tires more easily.

It doesn't happen in a day. Maybe you're looking at pictures of your dog, now 10, when he was a puppy. In the picture, he's leaping in the air to grab a Frisbee. You can actually see his waist, and maybe even the outline of a rib or two. You look at your dog now, snoozing by the TV. The only thing that's going to make him jump up is the promise of another snack.

You and your dog are not alone. According to a study conducted by Veterinary Pet Insurance, the United States' largest pet insurer, between 25 and 40 percent of the American pet population are overweight or obese. This has led to a big spike in obesity-related diseases such as diabetes and heart disease. Actuarial data compiled from Veterinary Pet Insurance in 2003 reveals that their clients' heart-related claims have risen more than 47 percent in the past two years.

It's not surprising that our dogs are getting fatter, not more fit; their owners are, too. As a nation, we're moving less and eating more. Dogs have to follow our lead. Even if they wanted to, dogs can't go out and shop for healthier food, or take themselves on extra walks.

Extra weight stresses your dog's system in ways you can't see until it's very far along. Overweight dogs are more prone to arthritis, diabetes, and heart problems.

DISEASES AND CONDITIONS ASSOCIATED WITH BEING OVERWEIGHT

What health impact does extra weight have on your dog? As with humans, it can exacerbate a number of diseases and conditions. It can, in some cases, bring them on earlier; in other cases, it makes the condition more severe. That's the bad news. The good news is that in many cases, if you manage your dog's weight when he's still a puppy, you may lessen or even avoid some health problems entirely. For instance, if you reduce your chubby female while she's still a puppy, when she's a mama dog about to give birth, she will have a much easier pregnancy. If you make sure that your dog sticks to a low-fat diet, he is far less like to have a bout of pancreatitis than the dog who scarfs fatty scraps under the table.

Arthritis

Arthritis, or degenerative joint disease, will affect at least 20% of all dogs during their lifetime. The symptoms—stiffness, lameness, and joint pain— are well known. Any extra poundage exacerbates the symptoms; one of the smartest, kindest things you can do is reduce your arthritic dog's weight.

Arthritis is diagnosed by X-raying your dog's joints. Frequently, your vet will recommend buffered aspirin, nutraceutical supplements such as glucosamine and chondroitin, or anti-inflammatory medications. Gentle physical therapy, particularly swimming, can also be helpful.

Diabetes

Diabetes occurs in dogs when the dog's body either doesn't produce enough insulin, or develops insensitivity to it. Without adequate insulin, your dog cannot control the production of glucose, the body's main fuel. This means that glucose, rather than being converted to energy, rises in the bloodstream and leaks into urine. Lacking fuel, your dog's body begins to feed on itself, breaking down fat and muscle, which generally means that your dog will continue to lose weight while his appetite rises. Other symptoms include excessive thirst and excessive urination.

With early diagnosis (via a blood test) and treatment, your dog can live well, following a daily regimen of a monitored, vet-prescribed diet, insulin injections, and glucose monitoring. But your dog's diet must be strictly regimented in order to stabilize his insulin requirements. Reducing the weight of your fat dog, under the supervision of a vet, will improve his quality of life.

Heart Disease and Heart Failure

According to the American Veterinary Medical Association Web site, of all the dogs examined annually by vets in the U.S., approximately 3.2 million will have some form of acquired heart disease, that is, a heart disease that is not present at birth. Obesity is one of the contributing factors to acquired heart disease, which typically damages either the heart valves or the muscular walls of the dog's heart. Eventually, untreated heart disease leads to heart failure, where the heart becomes unable to pump adequate blood through the body. Typical symptoms include lethargy, coughing, labored breathing, and, in the latter stages of heart failure, exercise intolerance and fainting. To definitively diagnose heart disease, your vet may use X-rays, blood and urine tests, and EKGs. Treatment depends on the nature and severity of the heart disease, and generally includes weight management, drugs, and surgery.

Hip Dysplasia

Hip dysplasia is a malformation of the hip joint, particularly common in medium- to large-size dogs, especially purebreds. This leads to looseness in the hip joints, causing cartilage damage, which frequently leads to arthritis and joint pain. It is diagnosed through X-rays.

Hip dysplasia is the most common cause of rear leg lameness in dogs. Obesity and overfeeding can contribute to the seriousness of the condition. Overfeeding large breed puppies can and does exacerbate the severity of this disease, causing the puppies to grow too quickly, which leads to early onset of hip dysplasia and arthritis.

Depending on the severity of the disease, dogs can be made to feel more comfortable through anti-inflammatories and non-weight bearing exercise such as swimming. For dogs who don't respond to drugs or physical therapy, a variety of surgical options are available, including hip replacement.

Pancreatitis

Pancreatitis occurs in dogs when the pancreas, an organ responsible for providing digestive enzymes and manufacturing insulin, becomes inflamed. Symptoms include, but are not restricted to, vomiting, lost of appetite, and abdominal pain. Dogs on high-fat diets and over-weight spayed females are more likely to suffer from pancreatitis. Symptoms can include vomiting, diarrhea, dehydration, and shock.

Pancreatitis has multiple causes, but it appears that a bout of pancreatitis can be brought on by a rich, fatty meal. Treatment includes putting the dog on a water, food, and oral medication fast for at least 24 hours (to "rest" the pancreas) while administering an intravenous saline solution.

Most mild forms of pancreatitis resolve themselves following treatment, but a dog who experiences extreme pancreatitis can suffer permanent pancreas damage and develop diabetes. Overweight dogs are particularly at risk; putting your dog on a low-fat, low-calorie diet can play an important part in preventing a first incident or a recurrence.

Prolonged or Difficult Labor

Prolonged or difficult labor occurs more frequently in overweight pregnant dogs, and often puts both the mother and puppies at risk. Doctors sometimes administer drugs to encourage labor, or manually correct the position of the puppies in the mother's womb so that the puppies can be expelled. When these techniques fail, vets must perform a cesarean section to remove the puppies. Unfortunately, when the c-section is performed after a long, difficult labor, complications can make this surgery risky for the mother and her surviving puppies.

Oversnacking and undermoving today mean much larger vet bills 5 or 10 years in the future—and, frankly, a more miserable dog. In many cases, it also means that your dog's life will be shorter.

But it's a trend that can be reversed, and here's the good news: It's probably easier for a dog to lose weight than his owner.

OKAY...MAYBE MY DOG ISN'T FAT, SHE'S JUST BIG-BONED

Maybe you're not ready to admit to your dog's fatness. It's okay. But if you're not sure, there's a reliable test to tell you whether your dog is carrying a little extra, and you don't even need a scale to carry it out. It goes without saying that you should take your pudgy pooch to the vet for a full evaluation, but if you have just a minute, you can get a better idea of how big Bowser really is.

But how exactly did this happen?

Probably the same way that humans gain weight—gradually, almost without noticing. Take the quiz on the next page to get a snapshot of the beliefs and behaviors that might have contributed to your dog's current weight gain.

Note: About This Book's "Just One Fat Minute"

Throughout this book, you'll have the opportunity to use "Just One Fat Minute"'s as tools to leading your dog to a healthier, skinnier life. See the next page for an example.

Just One Fat Minute: How to Assess your Pooch's Pudge

THIN

FIT

FAT

1.   The first part of the test involves touch. Run your hand along your dog's rib cage and feel his ribs. Ideally, you should be able to feel and count each one of them under the slightest layer of flesh.

2.   The second part of the test involves sight. Stand above your dog while he is standing on all four paws and take a good look at his torso. Right after the ribcage ends, and before the hips begin, his body should have an indentation—a nipped-in waist. While he may not have the contoured abs of a pop music star, you should be able to point to your dog's waist.

If you can't feel his ribs and you can't see his waist, then…your dog is officially too fat.

WHAT, MY DOG FAT? ASSESSMENT QUIZ

1.   My dog gets a total of _____ minutes of exercise per day.
2.   My dog gets a total of ____cups of food per day, and __ snacks.
3.   I know exactly who is feeding my dog, what my dog is being fed, and when. True or False?

4. When dogs get old, they're bound to put on weight. True or False?

5. Certain breeds are just "born chubby." True or False?

6. My dog just intuitively knows what to eat, and how much. True or False?

7. But my dog just looks so cute; I just have to give him a treat. True or False?

Answers

1. The typical dog needs a minimum of 30 minutes of exercise, i.e., walking, a day. That isn't much—that's half an "American Idol" or "Amazing Race." And that's walking. Not running or racing or rallying. Just plain walking. If you find yourself so overloaded that you can't walk your dog for that amount of time, seriously consider hiring a dog walker. Your dog will thank you in the future, and your vet bills will be lower.

2. The amount of food a dog requires depends on his age, size, and activity level. But the bottom line is this: You should be measuring your dog's food intake, even if he isn't overweight. And if he is overweight, using measuring cups is a simple reminder to begin cutting back.

3. Especially in the high-speed lives we lead now, it is very likely that more than one person in your household is responsible for feeding and exercising your dog. And, if your household is typical, that means that there may be a Good Cop/Bad Cop

team taking care of your dog in the same day. The Bad Cop measures out diet kibble and takes Fifi on a forced march. The Good Cop bounds home with extra treats from the pet store, then throws some food in a bowl, and gives the dog a short walk because he has a game he wants to watch. Dieting dogs in the suburbs or the country may have another food and exercise hurdle—the neighbors may enjoy playing with them AND feeding them. So, if you're being strict about your dog's exercise and diet regime, but he's still not losing weight, enlist your neighbors in your efforts.

4. When dogs get older, they often require fewer calories. But as far as exercise goes, just as with humans, much of what passes for "age" in dogs is actually lack of use, or underlying chronic physical problems, such as arthritis. Many of these problems can be alleviated, or even eliminated, with medications, more moderate exercise, or supplements.

5. Some breeds are more prone to extra pudge than others; the roly-poly retriever is nearly a cliché, while it's rare to see a chunky greyhound. These heftier breeds include: Labrador retrievers, Cairn terriers, cocker spaniels, long-haired dachshunds, Shetland sheepdogs, basset hounds, and beagles. That's why it's especially important, if you've just adopted a puppy from one of these born-to-bulge breeds, to start right now to keep your dog on the slim side.

6. This belief falls under the Myth of the SuperIntelligent Dog, promulgated by cartoons and movies. In the real

world, dogs do know what to eat: nearly everything, nearly all the time. Through thousands of years of evolution when food was generally scarce, dogs have learned to eat wherever, whenever—so much so that they are classified as omnivores. In the modern world, food is no longer scarce, but dogs' eating habits have not yet evolved to absorb that fact. (In fact, neither have ours!) So it's up to you, as a concerned owner, to control the supply.

7. This isn't necessarily a bad excuse, if you redefine what you mean by the world "cute." Start making your (cute) dog earn his treat by doing something for it. Begin to embrace the idea that, at least as far as your dog is concerned, Nothing In Life Is Free (NILIF for short). Before treating your dog, ask for a behavior, whether it is a sit, a stay, or a shake. Only treat when the dog provides what you've asked for, and make sure that the treats are healthy. It isn't necessary to go cold turkey on your chunky canine. You can start slow and mix in baby carrots or apple slices along with the usual liver treats. Eventually, you can give the dog variable reinforcement—one treat after every four acts of good behavior, as opposed to after every one. Your dog will always be cute; you just have to find a different way to reward the cuteness.

Okay, One Last Excuse: Could It Be Hormonal?

It could be. But it's probably not. Before you begin blaming your dog's pudginess on metabolic mayhem, remember this: Only a small percentage of dogs truly suffer from what could be called hormonal imbalances, and obesity is usually only one symptom among several serious ones.

Metabolic imbalances such as Cushing's syndrome (which gives a dog a distinctively bloated belly) or hypothyroidism (which causes weight gain in the dog) don't just make your dog fat. They wreak havoc with other parts of the dog's behavior and appearance—a dog with a metabolic problem such as hypothyroidism usually moves lethargically and often suffers from skin and coat problems. If this is the case with your dog, put this book down, get to a vet as soon as you can. This book is not for you.

This book is for you if your dog is, bluntly, fat and happy, with a bounce in his step—if a slightly slower one than he used to have. A fat dog with a shiny coat and peppy gait is not a candidate for a thyroid condition. That's a dog that's been snacking too much, and moving too little.

HOW MUCH SHOULD MY DOG WEIGH, ANYWAY?

The following are a list of some of the most popular breeds and their typical healthy adult weights. What's that, you say? Your dog's not typical? Your dog is a blend of beagle and Corgi and, well, maybe Basenji? Read on. No dog is typical, but these numbers give you a good place to start.

Your Dog's Weight in Pounds	
American Cocker Spaniel	24–28
Beagle	20–25
Boxer	55–70
Bulldog	50–55
Chihuahua	2–6
Dalmatian	50–55
Golden Retriever	60–80
Greyhound	60–70
Jack Russell Terrier	9–15
Labrador Retriever	55–75
Poodle	Toy 14–16.5
	Miniature 26–30
	Medium 30–42
Pug	14–18
Rhodesian Ridgeback	65–85
Rottweiler	90–110
Shih Tzu	10–16
St. Bernard	110–200
Yorkshire Terrier	5–7

If you've adopted your dog as a puppy, when should you be using a target adult weight to evaluate your dog? The answer is: It depends. Different breeds age at very different rates. While an "average" 1-year-old dog is basically a typical teenager—16 years old in terms of behavior and physical maturity—some small breed dogs reach puberty at five months, while some large breed females don't go into heat until they're about 18 months old. However, at the age of two, your dog, regardless of its breed, can be considered an adult. If your dog was at a healthy weight at two, that can be a good goal weight to shoot for.

Regardless of age or breed, if you suspect your dog is putting on weight, the first step always is to evaluate him based on a quick visual and tactile scan. From the side and above your dog, look for definition in his waistline, the area right below the ribs. Touch your dog's ribcage, and feel for his ribs; you should be able to feel them easily beneath a layer of fat. When in doubt, consult your vet to establish a target ideal weight for your dog.

SO IF YOU'RE READY....

If you bought this book, or someone gave you this book, congratulations! You've taken your first step on the road to a leaner canine. While it's a good idea to read the whole book, the book also provides advice in bite-size chunks. If you only have a minute to help your dog get skinny—that's still an important minute, and you should use it. If you have five minutes, you'll get even more help.

And a few minutes is enough. Despite the avalanche of information about canine weight loss out there, it isn't rocket science. Dogs, like humans, lose weight when they eat less and move more. Dogs, like humans, need encouragement and structure for this to happen. The good news is, unless you have a very unusual dog, it's a lot easier to structure your dog's eating and exercise habits than it is your own. Dogs don't have to skip their aerobics classes to drive their kids to a soccer match. Dogs don't get invited to parties where the snacks are just too good to resist. Dogs DO suffer from boredom, and when given the opportunity, will overeat if the food is put in front of them.

Dogs are not future-oriented creatures, but you can use this to your advantage. They don't go on diets because they want to look good for their tenth anniversary obedience school reunion. They go on diets because YOU help them do it. They go five or ten more minutes on their walks because you want them to and because they love you.

HOW LONG BEFORE I SEE RESULTS?

It depends on how fat your dog is. Just as with humans, the fatter your dog is, the faster he or she will probably lose weight in the beginning. Keep in mind that your dog should lose no more than 2% of his current weight per week. (On average, for a dog six years and older, the percentage should be no more than 1.5%.) For a 50-pound dog, that's exactly 1 pound. Unless you own a giant breed dog, you are going to see the victory in ounces, not pounds. That may take a little getting used to, but as your dog loses weight, you'll also see gradual but satisfying improvements in the dog's activity level, energy, even agility. The key to dog weight loss is the same one humans need in their own exercise and diet programs. They need to be patient. They need to celebrate little victories. So let's get started.

THE SKINNY ON THIS CHAPTER

- Most dogs are fat because they eat too much and exercise too little (that's the good news). In the United States, this affects at least one quarter of all dogs.
- Most healthy dogs can lose weight if they eat less and move more (that's the better news!).
- Before embarking on a weight loss program for your dog, make sure you take him to the vet for a complete checkup.
- Adult dogs should lose no more than 2% of their body weight per week. (For dogs weighing less than 50 pounds. that means we're talking ounces, not pounds.)
- Any weight loss program, whether it's for you or your dog, is likely to be more successful if you make it a team effort. Enlist your vet, your significant other, your friends, and your neighbors in Operation Reduce Rover.

Prepare for Your Vet Visit

First things first. If you are really serious about getting your dog to lose weight, it begins with taking him to the vet. No ifs, ands, or buts.

If you suspect that your dog may have a metabolic problem that's contributing to his weight problem, take him to the vet.

If you suspect that your dog may have food allergies, take him to the vet.

If you fear that your dog may have some physical issues that preclude him from exercising, take him to the vet.

You wouldn't put yourself on a weight loss plan without getting checked out first, would you? So why would you expect your dog to?

BEST KEPT VET SECRETS

Vets really do want to help your dog lose weight. Some vets come right out and tell you that your dog is too big. Still other vets may choose not to broach the weighty subject because current compliance is so low. Remember, estimates now claim from 25 percent to 40 percent of North America's pets are overweight. That means that at the kindest estimate, out of every four dogs visiting the vet's office, one is overweight.

Vets have read owners the riot act in the past, only to see it fail time and time again. It's certainly discouraging to see a fat human fail at a diet—in fact, it's human nature to deep-six a diet. But, because it could be so different, it may feel far worse to watch a dog fall victim to weight-related illnesses just because an owner overfeeds her Fido and barely gives him the walks he needs.

If you're really committed, let your vet know. Most vets want to be your partner in keeping your dog trim, so make sure you make it clear that this is important to you. Ohio-based vet Dr. Jennifer Jellison, D.V.M., participant in a recent study of weight loss and exercise in dogs AND their owners, tries to turn this problem into an opportunity. Much like a Weight Watchers instructor, she asks pet owners to show her what one cup of food actually looks like. They usually vastly overestimate. Then she hands them the cup and asks them to measure it out.

Next, she'll ask, "Does your dog like vegetables?" Often, they say, pet owners automatically say no, when in fact, they haven't tried to spring any vegetables on their dogs. Dr. Jellison often offers vegetables to a patient dog in front of his owner just to begin the "conversion" process.

BEFORE YOU GO: THE DOG LOG

When you bring your dog to the vet to discuss his weight loss program, come armed with two things: information and questions. While your vet can weigh your dog and administer the appropriate tests, only you can accurately assess your dog's day to day eating and exercise patterns. Ideally, you'll have kept some kind of a log of your dog's food intake and exercise to discuss with your vet. Make it clear to your vet that you intend to really help your dog lose weight.

Researchers in human weight loss have found that one of the key components to consistent and permanent weight loss can be keeping track of what you eat and how much you move.

Until your dog learns how to type, you'll have to do it for him. The statistics you keep are simple: How much did your dog move, and how much did your dog eat? You can use the preprinted sheet, or develop your own Dog Log in a pocket-sized notebook, on your PDA, or computer. But simple and fast is usually best. If this is too much effort, you can use a wall calendar. The goal is to help you become more aware of what your dog's taking in, and how much he's moving. Even doing this for one day will have an influence on how you care for your dog.

Turn the page to see the Dog Log!

SAMPLE DOG LOG

HOW MANY WALKS?

1 __10__ minutes
2 __40__ minutes
3 __40__ minutes

COMMENTS: Morning walk cut short by rain. Gave Faith a longer walk in the afternoon, plus played "find my keys" for 10 minutes. Jeff said night walk was long—Faith played with friends.

HOW MANY MEALS? 2

Morning	Evening
2/3 cup lite food	2/3 cup lite food
plus cup grated carrots	plus flaxseed oil

HOW MANY SUPPLEMENTS?

1 scoop glucosamine powder

HOW MANY TREATS?

5 mini-bones

WHAT COOL THING DID MY DOG DO TODAY?

She did a backflip

WHAT AM I PLANNING FOR MY DOG TOMORROW?

I'm taking her to the park

YOUR DOG LOG

HOW MANY WALKS?

1_____minutes
2_____minutes
3_____minutes

COMMENTS: _____

_____

_____

HOW MANY MEALS?

Morning   Evening

_____

_____

HOW MANY SUPPLEMENTS?

_____

HOW MANY TREATS?

_____

WHAT COOL THING DID MY DOG DO TODAY?

_____

WHAT AM I PLANNING FOR MY DOG TOMORROW?

_____

QUESTIONS TO ASK YOUR VET

Make sure that you get the following questions answered.

What should my dog look like?

This is actually a little different from "how much should my dog weigh," though clearly weight is important. Some people read breed descriptions and worry because their dog falls to either side of the

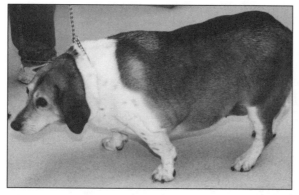

This overweight pooch is on his way to the vet.

standard description. Instead, ask your vet to show you how to examine your dog's waist from the top, and how to feel for your dog's ribs to make sure that he's eating right. Thanks to centuries of breeding, the "perfect physique" for dogs varies as widely as their breeds do. A big-chested American Staffordshire terrier, for instance, may look fat—but is actually carrying quite a bit of muscle along with its bulk. Long-haired breeds, from the traditional standard American poodle to the more recently popular Goldendoodle and Labradoodle may hide a fairly skinny frame beneath a thick, fluffy coat. This is where your vet comes in. He or she will have seen many, many more version of your dog's breed than you ever will. And while there is no such thing as a BMI index for dogs or cats (yet), your vet can tell you much more about the parameters of your dog's typical activity level and body weight. Some breeds really were born to run, and others were born to sit a lot.

How much food should I be feeding my dog?

Does my dog need a special diet? Once you have an accurate goal weight for your dog, discuss what the optimal fuel for him is. If possible, ask to see a sample portion for your dieting dog. If your doctor feels that your dog has any special nutritional issues, ask for food recommendations, or even a diet food available through his office.

How much exercise should my dog get daily?

The bare minimum for your adult dog should be three 15-minute walks a day. This may seem scarcely adequate for a frenetic puppy, and more of a serious challenge for a senior dog suffering from arthritis, or other illnesses. Especially in the beginning of a weight loss program, it's important to create a reachable target for your dog's exercise. This is also the time to discuss any special needs your dog might have due to age, medical history, or breed. Try, also, to discuss future goals for your dog's fitness.

How does my dog's breed affect his health?

Every dog is unique, and each dog breed contains a multitude of variations. However, there is no question that certain dogs are prone to overweight. Dr. Phil Brown, D.V.M., veterinary consultant to pet food companies and formerly a small animal vet on Cape Cod, Massachusetts, cautions owners of puppies of several breeds, including poodles and Labrador retrievers, to monitor their dogs' weight from an early age. Breeds that are prone to hip dysplasia, a malformation of the hip joint, need to be kept slim from puppydom. Flat-faced dogs such as pugs, bulldogs, and Pekingese should spend very little time outside in the summer heat, as they can easily suffer from heat stroke.

What kind of changes should I expect as my dog ages?

After your dog officially reaches middle age (as early as five for some dogs), it's vital that your dog get a complete workup every year, and, ideally, a dental cleaning under anesthesia. (Poor dental care can lead not just to bad breath and difficulty in eating, but bacteria from mouth infections can compromise the immune system and even infect your dog's heart valves.)

QUESTIONS YOUR VET WILL ASK YOU

Once you've gotten your questions answered, your vet will probably have some of his own. Keeping a Dog Log can really help to answer these, and you should bring one if you've been keeping it.

Have you noticed any changes in your dog's feeding or activity patterns?

Changes in these areas can be the tip-off to other health issues, from joint problems to hormonal imbalance. Even if it turns out that your dog is normal, it's important to have a conversation with your vet about what "normal" activity and eating look like, so that you're in agreement.

Do you measure your dog's food?
Do you know how much a cup of food is?

This is another part of establishing what "normal" looks like. Many dog lovers never measure their dog's food, or rely on the dog food label recommendations without taking into account the dog's activity level.

Who else feeds your dog?

Dr. Martha Gearhart, D.V.M., of the Pleasant Valley Animal Hospital of Pleasant Valley, New York, reports that well-meaning pet owners can be sabotaged by "the others," meaning friends, family members, and, in the case of dogs that have the run of the outside world, both neighbors and the outside (dog snack-filled) world. A vet visit can be the perfect time to assess just who else might be stuffing your dog full of treats. Discussing this with the vet gives you the opportunity to begin an action plan to convince the others to help you slim down your dog.

Who else takes care of your dog?

You may believe that when you leave your dog at home with family members, your dog scampers and plays. The reality may be something closer to this: Your well-meaning caretaker sits in a chair, watches television, and likes to feed the dog all day because it keeps the dog near. If you employ a dog walker, make it very clear that you expect your dog to be exercised and, if the dog goes to a dog run, encouraged to play hard. Really successful weight loss in a pet involves identifying all the factors and all the people who contribute to your dog's weight gain, and enlisting them in the campaign for change. This may not happen overnight, but it can happen.

Adopting a Dog

If you haven't actually selected your dog yet, this is a good time to do your research and discover just what a typical day for a Jack Russell terrier might look like, as opposed to a Rottweiler. The Internet and the bookstore are both excellent resources if you're still shopping around for a canine companion. If you're close enough to a dog park, spend a half an hour watching dogs interact with each other. You'll learn a lot. Ask every dog-owning friend probing questions. If you can, grill your local vet.

You'll learn a lot, and some of it will surprise you. While many people assume that a cute little dog will endure more confinement than a big lumbering breed, it isn't necessarily true. The terrier's job back in the day was hunting rats down tunnels and killing them. They would search out their prey for miles and miles. And though it's unlikely that you'd like your dog to be seeking and finding vermin, that genetic memory remains in the breed, as well as the hunger for physical activity. Meanwhile, larger breeds that have been bred to stand guard in one place may adapt well to inside, relatively sedentary life.

Know yourself. What kind of lifestyle are you currently leading? Are you a marathon runner, or a gentle walker? Do you love to tramp through the woods for miles with your dog? If you do, then you probably don't want a British bulldog, who can't generally spend lots of time outside because the breed is prone to heat stroke. On the other hand, if you dream of sitting in front of the computer, with a pile of love in your lap, take a pass on the border collie, shepherd extraordinaire, and look for a smaller, more sedentary lap dog breed, such as the Bichon Frise, Maltese, Lhasa apso, Pomeranian, or a pug. That's what they were bred for.

Are you ready to change?

Dr. Gearhart admits that the first thing she does when discussing a dog's weight problem is look at the owner. If the dog is fat and the owner is of average size, she says, then it's generally easy to enlist the owner. If the owner is maintaining a healthy weight, she encourages, then isn't it time to help the dog get there, too?

Keep in mind that even positive change is stressful. Go slow and steady, and assume you will have setbacks. But don't let that stop you from taking care of your dog today.

Once your dog gets a good bill of health, thank your vet. Make an appointment for a follow-up visit in a few months. Ideally, you'll be bringing back a thinner, healthier dog.

THE SKINNY ON THIS CHAPTER

- Never start a diet and exercise program for your dog without taking him to the vet first.
- Come prepared with questions to ask your vet during the visit.
- Ask for your vet's support while slimming down your dog.
- If you haven't yet chosen a dog, use a vet visit to discuss what kind of dog is optimal for your lifestyle.

Rule Out Other Health Problems

Though the vast majority of overweight dogs are fat for the usual reasons—too much food and too little exercise—there's no question that dogs can and do gain weight due to a variety of medical conditions. Some of these conditions, such as false pregnancy, are common in dogs, and not life-threatening. Others, such as bloat, are immediate medical emergencies.

HYPOTHYROIDISM

If you have any concerns regarding your dog's thyroid activity, by all means, ask your vet to evaluate your pet. Remember: Extra poundage by itself is rarely a symptom of an underactive thyroid gland in a dog.

Dogs suffering from genuine hypothyroidism, aka a sluggish metabolism, don't just look fat. They have a whole cluster of symptoms. They move like molasses. They seem slightly disconnected from the world. They suffer from lethargy, weight gain, and hair loss. The cause is a lack of thyroid production.

The primary diagnostic test for hypothyroidism is called the T4. Retesting is often necessary because hormone levels can rise and fall in perfectly healthy dogs. Further tests may be necessary to definitively determine the disease. Once again, remember: If the dog is overweight, but alert and active, it isn't hypothyroidism.

Dogs who have hypothyroid condition will need a lifetime daily dose of synthetic thyroid hormone, as well as periodic testing.

CUSHING'S DISEASE

Another metabolic condition found to cause overweight in dogs is Cushing's Disease, or hyperadrenocorticism. Cushing's occurs when your dog's adrenal glands produce too much of the hormone cortisol. In 85% of the cases, this is caused by a tiny, usually benign tumor in the pituitary gland, which causes the gland to secrete a hormone, ACTH, which in turn makes the adrenal glands overproduce cortisol. This disease is also known as PDH. In 15% of the cases, the disease is a result of a tumor on the adrenal gland, which causes an overproduction of cortisol.

Again, while testing is required to determine whether your dog actually has this condition, dogs who suffer from Cushing's generally display a host of symptoms, not simply excess weight. Symptoms of Cushing's include an increase in thirst and urination, sluggishness, thin skin, a distinctively bloated belly, panting, and bilateral symmetrical hair loss. Definitively diagnosing Cushing's often requires a number of tests, including blood count, urinanalysis, serum chemistry profile, as well as hormone tests such as ACTH-stimulation and low dose dexamethacone screening. When PDH Cushing's is diagnosed, it is usually treated with a lifelong regimen of drugs. When Cushing's is a result of an adrenal tumor, surgery is performed to remove the tumor.

ASCITES

Ascites is the abnormal accumulation of fluid in the abdomen, causing your dog to look pot-bellied. When your dog suffers from ascites, if you tap your dog's abdomen, it will give off a dull thump. Because it can be a symptom of a number of different illnesses, including Cushing's syndrome (see above) congestive heart failure, kidney disease, liver failure, heartworm, or ovarian tumors, take your dog to the vet as soon as you notice it.

BLOAT (GASTRIC DILATION VOLVULUS)

If your dog's stomach suddenly appears bloated, treat it as a medical emergency. Bloat is a life-threatening emergency that develops very suddenly, usually in a healthy dog, with a ferociously high mortality rate—killing almost 50% of the dogs who suffer from it. If you suspect that your dog is suffering from bloat, take your dog immediately to a veterinary hospital.

A large and deep-chested dog who eats too much and too fast is at particular risk for bloat. Bloat generally develops after a dog has quickly eaten a large meal, exercised intensely before or after a meal, or drunk a lot of water immediately after eating. The stomach can distend with gas and fluid, causing gastric dilation. Bloat can also set off a second condition, known as volvulus, where the stomach rotates, causing gas and fluids to become trapped. This prevents the dog from belching and vomiting, which can lead to a number of life-threatening conditions. A dog suffering from bloat appears anxious, often drooling, retching, and pacing. Eventually, the dog's midsection swells. Treatment usually involves relieving the pressure through a stomach tube, or large needle, followed by surgery to correct the rotation of the stomach.

FALSE PREGNANCY

False pregnancy is a fairly common condition in dogs. It is caused by progesterone, manufactured by corpora luteal cysts in the ovaries, and occurs about six to eight weeks after the dog has gone into heat. A "pseudopregnant" dog can demonstrate all the symptoms of an actual pregnancy, including an enlarged abdomen, nausea, distended nipples, and even lactation. Pseudopregnant dogs may even build a nest, and become fiercely protective of toys or other puppy substitutes. In most cases, the false pregnancy disappears after approximately 12 weeks. In a small number of cases, dogs with severe symptoms, such as abnormal aggression or caked mammary glands, may require a mild tranquilizer, or a course of hormonal therapy.

PREGNANCY

If you've decided not to spay your female dog, and she's an adult, and she suddenly seems to put on weight, she may just be pregnant. Canine pregnancies typically last an average of 63 days from the start of ovulation. In the first month of a dog's pregnancy, a healthy, pregnant dog will gain a little weight, and may experience morning sickness. If you've intentionally bred your dog, take her to the vet two to three weeks after breeding. If you suspect that your dog has accidentally become pregnant, take her to the vet. Later on, the symptoms will become more obvious. During the second half of a dog's pregnancy, her breasts enlarge and the belly stretches. Your vet can locate the presence of puppies in early pregnancy by palpating the abdomen, or throughout the pregnancy via ultrasound. In late pregnancy, your dog's belly will grow and hang very low. Make sure to monitor your dog's weight throughout the whole exciting process. If your dog gains too much during pregnancy, she may experience a difficult labor, endangering herself and her puppies.

THE SKINNY ON THIS CHAPTER

- Sudden, unexplained weight gain can be caused by a minor health issue-or can constitute a life-threatening emergency.
- Metabolic conditions such as hypothyroidism and Cushing's syndrome affect the whole dog, from personality to skin tone-weight gain is only one of the symptoms.
- Bloat, which causes the dog's stomach to swell from gas and fluid, is a fast-moving and frequently lethal medical emergency.
- A false pregnancy can cause your female dog's stomach to swell, but it is not a serious issue.
- When your dog really is pregnant, monitoring her weight is key to an easy pregnancy and safe delivery.

Learn What to Feed Your Dog

Just as in the human world, the search for the perfect dog diet never ends. Walk down the aisles of any pet supply store, and you're likely to be overwhelmed by the choices available. And that doesn't even include what your vet may prescribe if your dog suffers from an illness or has become a senior dog. It's just not possible to be comprehensive. What follows in this chapter are some basics to get you started on the road to a thinner, fitter dog.

THE BASICS

The nutritional building blocks of dog food are the same that make up human food. Like us, dogs are omnivores, which means they can, and on occasion, do, eat almost anything and turn it into fuel. (In practical terms, this means that unlike cats, dogs can eat a vegetarian diet.) Dog food, regardless of form or origin, should be made up of fat, protein, carbohydrates, fiber, vitamins, and minerals. Use these guidelines to help translate the dog food label, or, in the case of making your dog's food, creating nutritional targets.

DRY VS. WET?

On average, canned dog foods supply about 500 calories in a pound of food. Moist or chunky dog food has approximately 1,300 calories, while dry kibble has 1,600. Which should you choose? You may make a choice based on looks, but keep in mind: Your dog's primary guide to good food is his nose. Humans have around 12,000 taste buds, but dogs boast only about 2,000. When given taste tests, dogs do show preferences, so, when deciding to diet your dog, do pick something he's going to enjoy.

When choosing a dog food, ask yourself:

- How old is my dog?
- How active?
- How convenient is this food?

Some owners choose canned food, for instance, because it offers a premeasured amount—but keep in mind that may not be the amount that you want to offer your dog. Canned may also be the way to go if you like to travel with your dog, and don't want to schlep around a giant bag of dog food. Kibble, on the other hand, is easy to measure.

WHO OVERSEES YOUR DOG'S FOOD?

The Association of American Feed Control Officials (AAFCO) is the voluntary regulatory body overseeing what goes into your dog's food. AAFCO sets the nutritional standards that you see on dog food labels. AAFCO offers two ways to "pass" their standard, and one is preferable to the other.

The first way is based on a purely chemical analysis of the nutrients in your dog's food. Some joke that, using this standard, a shoe filled with motor oil could meet the AAFCO chemical standards. While it's a joke, it's an important consideration when thinking about feeding your dog. The chemical standard does not ask that the source of the food be of high quality, only that it meet the chemical requirements for a healthy balanced diet. Just because it can doesn't necessarily mean it should.

The second preferred AAFCO standard is based on feeding trials with real live dogs. To pass the feeding trials, manufacturers feed their products to dogs to assure that the products maintain canine good health. This is a more "real world" test, and definitely the one you should be looking for when shopping for dog food.

However, this standard is far from perfect. Feeding trials are of short duration, typically lasting six months. The ideal food trial, some say, would last two years and span two complete generations of dogs, in order to certify that the food was appropriate and healthy throughout a dog's lifespan. This is an expensive and time-consuming process which most companies have not yet adopted.

LABELS MATTER

To find out just what kind of testing your dog food has undergone, start with the label. Some companies describe precisely what kind of testing they've performed on their foods. If that's not available, call them up and ask them. You owe it to your dog.

The bottom line is, regardless of the brand you ultimately choose, make sure that the label assures you that the food provides "Complete and Balanced Nutrition."

WHAT ARE A DOG FOOD'S BUILDING BLOCKS?

Fat. Fat provides over twice as many calories per gram as carbohydrates or protein. Clearly, your fat dog needs less fat in his diet, but he still needs some, in order to ingest fat soluble vitamins (A, D, E, and K), essential fatty acids, and others. Fat content in a dieting adult dog's dry dog food should range between 5-12%.

Protein. Even if your dog must lose weight, adequate protein is vital to prevent his losing lean body mass. Look for a dry food that offers at least 25% crude protein.

Fiber. A typical diet dog food will contain a high level of fiber. Along with helping to stabilize the dog's blood glucose level and improving the body's sensitivity to insulin, fiber encourages your dog to chew, and slows the rate of movement of food out of the stomach. In short, it makes your dog feel more "full." Diet foods usually contain at least 5% fiber, all the way up to 30%. Be aware that a very high-fiber diet can cause flatulence and increase the amount of a dog's stool.

Vitamins and minerals. It's vital that when you reduce your dog's calories, you don't reduce access to vitamins and minerals. Vitamins are divided into two categories: water soluble and fat soluble. Water soluble vitamins include the B vitamins, niacin, panthothenic acid, folic acid, biotin, choline, and vitamin C. Fat soluble vitamins are vitamins A, D, E, and K.

Dog-necessary minerals are potassium, magnesium, zinc, calcium, iron, phosphorus, sodium, chloride, among others. They are a small, but essential part of your dog's diet.

ARE SUPPLEMENTS NECESSARY?

It's likely, if your dog eats a conventional AAFCO-approved dog food that he's getting an adequate amount of vitamins and minerals. Before you decide that your dog needs vitamin or mineral supplements, discuss it with your vet. It is possible to overdose your dog on fat-soluble vitamins, which are not flushed out of the dog's system the way water-soluble vitamins are. On the other hand, more and more vets are recommending glucosamine and chondroitin as extra protection against arthritis, even with younger dogs. However, because these are supplements, not drugs, keep in mind that they fall under no regulatory body, and the quality can vary greatly.

Just Five Fat Minutes

Buy a bag of organic carrots. Grate one up and add to your dog's food.

DO YOU REALLY NEED A DIET DOG FOOD FOR YOUR FAT DOG?

More and more, when you shop for food for your dog, you'll see pet food formulas seemingly targeted at dogs who are overweight. There are "light" formulas, as well as "low-fat" and "reduced calorie" formulas. What do these labels mean, and will they really help your dog?

Fortunately, AAFCO now regulates these definitions, so if you buy a dry dog food meeting AAFCO standards for "light," you can be sure that it contains no more than 3100 calories per kilogram (2.2 pounds). According to AAFCO standards for light dog foods, a kilogram of semi-moist food must contain no more than 2500, and a canned food of the same portion will have no more than 900 calories. Under AAFCO guidelines, low-fat dog food must meet specific fat levels: low-fat dry food has a maximum of 9% fat, semi-moist contains a maximum of 7% fat, and canned food can contain up to 4% fat.

Finally, a "reduced calorie" version of a dog food of any type must indicate by what percentage its calories are reduced, compared to the dog food company's regular brand and in the same moisture-content category. For instance, "Pretty Pooches' Reduced Calorie Lamb and Rice— 25% fewer calories than Pretty Pooches' Regular Lamb and Rice."

So…does it make sense to buy lite, low-fat, or reduced calorie dog food? It's a qualified maybe. Are you prone to eat more low-fat cookies just because they're low-fat? Are you casual about portion control because it's too much hassle? Chances are, those habits are making your dog fat—not his food. Any dog food will make your dog fat if you feed him too much of it. Simply buying a bag of diet dog food won't make your dog thinner. Restricting his calories will. However, if you have a finicky dog who is unusually partial to a particular brand of dog food, you might want to invest in the "reduced calorie" version of it to ease the transition—assuming that he doesn't notice the difference. If you have strong feelings about feeding your dog low-fat meals, then take advantage of the low-fat options. Remember that dogs still need healthy fats in their diets, so don't cut back too much.

SHOULD YOU GO MORE NATURAL?

There's a very good reason to choose commercially-produced dog food for your furry friend. It's convenient, and it's consistent. Assuming that you have checked the label, you can be reasonably sure that what you're giving your dog is what he'll be eating. In order to represent its product as "complete," "balanced," "perfect," "scientific," "for all life stages," or "formulated for growth, pregnancy, or lactation," a company must adhere to specific AAFCO standards.

But it's impossible to ignore the controversy, and the growing literature, that deals with the idea that the best diet for your dog is a more "natural" one. Just what does that mean?

The controversy embraces a number of issues. Current standards are broad enough so that protein in dog food, for instance, can come from high-quality organic lamb, for example—or meat by-products, poultry by-products, fish by-products, soybean meals, and cereal grains, which may lack both quality and digestibility.

Another issue is the labeling loophole that allows a dog food label to list an appealing ingredient such as "beef," or "chicken," while the food itself contains as little as 3% of the item listed. Yet another popular criticism is of the various food processing methods used to create dog food, which can diminish the food sources' original nutritional value.

Many smaller, "natural" pet food companies have sprung up in the midst of this heated conversation. For example, the founders of the Blue Buffalo Company of Wilton, Connecticut, were inspired by the fight against cancer that CEO Bill Bishop's Airedale, Blue, went through—three times. The search for high quality ingredients to help maintain Blue's health led to the creation of Blue Buffalo, a cat and dog food company advised by Dr. Bob Goldstein, D.V.M., a holistic vet based in Westport, Connecticut, Medical Director of the Healing Center for Animals, and developer of a nutritional blood test for animals. Blue Buffalo's food is made up of variety of natural ingredients, and processed in a way that its founders feel that the food retains more of its nutrients. It has been rated highly by Whole Dog Journal. The top two ingredients in their Life Protection Formula are a very healthy portion of protein in the form of human-grade deboned lamb and lamb meal, and also in the top ten are alfalfa, brown rice, and whole carrots.

If you're concerned about the source of your dog's chow, foods from smaller, more independent companies may be your preference, especially when you're concerned about the quality of the calories your dog is consuming. Be aware that the big pet food companies are aware of consumer demand for more natural pet food. According to spokesman Stephen Payne of the Pet Food Institute, the trade association of pet food manufacturers, "The Pet Food Institute has been working with the US Department of Agriculture's National Organic Standards Board on the development of organic rules for some time now."

WHAT EXACTLY DOES MY DOG NEED TO EAT?
As a Puppy

During the first year of your puppy's life, he requires double the amount of calories per pound of body weight that he will as an adult. His protein requirements are much higher, too. Developmentally speaking, your puppy zooms from 0 to 16 in the first year of his life, from infant to teenager. Nourish accordingly!

When feeding your puppy, look for dog food that is labeled either for puppies or for all stages of life. This is a critical period of your dog's nutritional life, and you can't afford to get it wrong. A typical dry puppy food should meet the following requirements:

- 25% protein
- 17% fat
- less than 5% fiber
- 1.0–1.8% calcium
- 80% digestible
- 1750 metabolizable calories per pound of food

When Does Your Dog Like to BARF?

In some animal circles, it's all the rage, despite its somewhat questionable acronym: the BARF diet.

BARF stands for Bones and Raw Food, or, alternately, Biologically Appropriate Raw Food. The ingredients in the diet include raw, meaty bones, and vegetables, and are what we assume dogs ate in the wild before they were tamed. Many pet owners swear by this regimen, even though it takes more preparation than buying a bag of dog food. Proponents of the diet argue that modern dog food contains cooked grains and meat, which were never part of an ancestral dog's diet; they also question the quality of the meat going into dog food. Critics of the diet argue that raw meat attracts bacteria, that the BARF-based diet does not include enough nutrients, and finally, that the data supporting BARF's superiority just isn't strong enough. If you are interested in exploring this diet for your dog, do your research.

During the first six months of your puppy's life, feed him three times a day. After six months, twice a day is sufficient. At one year, keep to that feeding schedule—but switch your dog over to an adult food. Your puppy is no longer growing at a fast and furious rate, and doesn't need the same level of calories or nutrients.

The amount of food your puppy eats clearly should be based on both weight and breed, along with any other special considerations. If your puppy belongs to a large breed, it is vital that you not overfeed him. Overfeeding your big puppy can lead to the onset of serious health issues later, such as hip dysplasia and joint-related problems. When it comes to a large breed pup, slow, steady, and lean are the way to go.

As an Adult Dog

Your dog's nutritional target is as unique as he is. However, here are some basic bottom lines:

- Fat content in a dieting adult dog's dry dog food should range between 5-12%.
- Look for a dry food that offers at least 25% crude protein.
- Diet foods usually contain at least 5% fiber, all the way up to 30%. Start conservatively, as a high-fiber dog can also be a flatulent dog.

Your Dog as a Senior Citizen

According to Dr. Aine McCarthy, D.V.M., director of veterinary marketing at Veterinary Pet Insurance, "Older dogs...have diminished basal metabolic rates, decreased cardiovascular, musculoskeletal and respiratory functions, decreases in muscle mass, and reduced immune responses. The drop in metabolic rate and the reduced activity levels as pets age mandate a reduction in caloric and fat intake. Nutrients such as protein, vitamins, and minerals that preserve lean tissue must be in proper levels with high availability."

What that means for a typical owner of a typical older dog is this: Keep the calories low while keeping the nutrients high. Look for food that will provide your older dog with the best possible mix of nutrients without overloading him with fat. The good news is that the pet food industry has responded to this audience with dog food that's tailored to the healthy older dog.

Pregnant Dogs: Eating For Two, Three, Four...Or More

Compared to humans, dogs are very efficient breeders. The average dog pregnancy lasts a brief 63 days.

But that still gives a dog plenty of time to gain too much weight. Unless your mama dog has shown other symptoms, there's little reason to restrict her activity until the final two weeks of her pregnancy—no roughhousing or climbing fences. That's just common sense.

In terms of diet, increase your pregnant dog's food gradually, but limit it to no more than 1.5 times the amount she was eating before she got pregnant. It's very tempting to project your fantasies about a pregnant dog's cravings...but don't. A 15-25 percent weight gain is average, and any more could actually put the puppies at risk. Overweight bitches seem to suffer more than the average whelping problems.

WHAT FOODS DOES MY DOG NEED TO AVOID?

Eventually, your dog is going to eat something he shouldn't. Every dog owner has heard the miracle story of The Golden Retriever Who Ate the Giant Cake and Was Just Fine. But have you ever actually met this dog? You will usually hear this story right after your dog has gobbled some chocolate, and the goal of the storyteller is to make you feel better. If your dog is large and the amount of chocolate he's eaten is small and not very concentrated (think milk chocolate rather than unsweetened bakers chocolate), you might get lucky, and then someone will be telling your lucky story. But then again, you might not.

Thanks to thousands of years of breeding, dogs are omnivores, which means, given the chance, they can and will eat almost anything. This probably evolved as a survival mechanism and has kept them alive. However this now means that dogs often eat things that can harm and even kill them. Here is a list of some of the more seriously dangerous foods and other substances. If you suspect your dog has been poisoned, call your vet immediately, and, if necessary, rush your dog to an emergency medical facility. You might not get a second chance.

Chocolate. Chocolate contains methylxanthines (caffeine and the alkaloid methylbromine), which are poisonous to dogs. While dogs rarely die from consuming chocolate, chocolate consumption can cause seizures and even coma. When the dog is small and the chocolate is not, you could have a lethal situation on your hands.

Coffee. Coffee contains caffeine, which is a methylxanthine, which is poisonous to your dog.

Grapes and raisins. Until recently, grapes came highly recommended as a healthy treat for dogs. However, based on 140 cases tracked by the ASPCA Animal Poison Control Center between 2003 and 2004, the evidence is growing that grapes (and therefore, raisins) attack the kidney. Overconsumption of grapes and raisins can cause anything from vomiting to kidney failure to death.

Chicken bones. Chicken bones, somewhat ubiquitous on urban streets and in suburban garbage cans, can shatter in your dog's throat or stomach, creating lethal ice pick-sharp edges. Even if this calamity doesn't occur, remember chicken bones that have been in the garbage often carry harmful bacteria.

Antifreeze. To dogs, it tastes very sweet. But it is deadly. Less than three ounces will kill a 40-pound dog. Make sure if you store antifreeze in your garage that it is properly sealed, and that none of your pets have access to it. If you discover your dog licking a pool of something under a car during a snowy walk, be better safe than sorry and contact your vet.

Human nonsteroidal anti-inflammatory drugs (NSAIDS). These are commonly known as aspirin, ibuprofen, naproxen, and ketoprofen. It may be tempting to administer a little human aspirin or ibuprofen to your dog after a long workout, but depending on the dosage, according to the ASPCA Animal Poison Control Center, the result could be gastrointestinal (GI) upset, ulceration and/or perforation of the GI tract, bleeding disorders, kidney damage and central nervous system effects such as loss of coordination, seizures, and coma. If you feel that your dog really needs a pain reliever, seek out your vet and have him prescribe one designed for dogs. Be careful not to leave pills or open bottles unattended on a counter.

Rodenticide. Certain kinds of rat and mouse poison, or rodenticides, contain an anticoagulant, which, if ingested by a dog, may cause spontaneous bleeding and eventually death. Dogs sometimes consume this poison indirectly when they eat a dead rodent. A second type of rodenticide elevates the level of calcium in the body, leading to seizures, and sometimes death.

Toxic plants. To get a full list of plants that can make your dog sick, log on to the ASPCA Animal Poison Center Web site, listed in the Resources in the back of this book. Here are a few of the bad and the ugly:

- American Yew
- Buttercup
- Castor bean
- Oleander
- Rhubarb
- Wisteria

If your dog has been poisoned, establish what it is your dog has ingested. Contact your vet immediately, and get your dog to an emergency vet service.

If it's appropriate, call the ASPCA Animal Poison Control Center: (888) 426-4435. This number is staffed around the clock with experienced vets. They also have an extensive collection of individual cases—more than 600,000—involving pesticide, drug, plant, metal, and other exposures in food-producing and companion animals. They can provide consultation and advice to your vet. Your credit card may be charged for the consultation (at the time of this writing, the fee is $50).

Meanwhile, make sure you have a basic animal first aid kit at home which includes a 3% peroxide solution, in case you need to induce vomiting in your dog, a muzzle, and an appropriate pet carrier, should you need to move your dog. Ideally, you'll never have to use it.

THE SKINNY ON THIS CHAPTER

- Thanks to consumer demand, more and more pet food companies are offering nutritionally complete and organic food that will also help your dog lose weight.
- Dogs' nutritional needs change as they age. If your puppy is overweight, it could subtract years from his life.
- While pregnant dogs need more nutrients, overfeeding may actually endanger them and their puppies.
- Dogs often eat things they shouldn't. Keep the phone number of the ASPCA Animal Poison Control Center on speed-dial and prepare a dog emergency first aid kit just in case.

Change How and When You Feed Your Dog

HOW MUCH SHOULD YOUR DOG EAT?

Getting your dog to lose weight nearly always boils down to two basic steps: Getting your dog to move more, and making sure he eats fewer calories.

However, as with human weight gain, your dog's excess pounds probably crept up on both him and you, because the bad health habits gradually outweighed the good. You stopped—or never started—measuring your dog's food. You let him eat human food at the table. You didn't limit snacks. You stopped—or never started—making him work for his food. So when reversing the process, take it slowly. Your dog didn't gain weight overnight, and he won't lose it that way, either. It takes time and patience to change. You'll be more successful in the long run if you modify your dog's diet gradually.

DOG DIETS

So what does a dog diet look like? In general, it looks just like a human diet. You make sure your dog is burning more calories than he's taking in. While you may not always be able to increase your dog's exercise each day, you can carefully control his food. What follows are some recommended food plans for different-sized dogs, based on existing sample diet dog foods—dry, semi-moist, and canned from a popular pet food company's Web site. However, you can and should design your own dog's diet, because each dog is different. Your dog may be much more active than the average 30-pound dog, for instance, and will need more calories. Or you may find you may need to limit your beagle's diet more than you expected, because Uncle Henry is never ever going to stop passing table scraps to Snoopy.

What is absolutely vital is that you measure two things: 1) your dog's weight (on a weekly basis), and 2) the caloric value of the food, in whatever form, that you give him on a daily basis. Without these measurements, you can't be sure of the progress you are making. Keep in mind, also, that these are all recommended amounts, and the calories do differ depending on the kind of food you're serving your dog. If you follow the recommended serving amounts from these dog foods, for instance, your 10-pound dog would be eating approximately 245 calories if you fed him either dry or canned food, but he'd be eating 273 calories' worth of the semi-moist food. For a 40-pound dog, the range of recommended food goes from 574 calories' worth of dry dog food to 609 canned to 682 in the semi-moist variety.

Dry Dog Food

Type: 8-ounce cup of weight control formula dry lamb meal and rice dog food, 328 calories/cup

Sample Diet 1

Dog's Weight: 30 pounds

Feeding instructions: 1-1/2 cups total daily. When goal weight is achieved, increase feeding to 1-3/4 cups.

Feeding frequency: First meal, 1 cup. Second meal, 1/2 cup.

Sample Diet 2

Dog's Weight: 60 pounds

Feeding instructions: 2-1/2 cups total daily. When goal weight is achieved, increase to 2-3/4 cups.

Feeding frequency: First meal, 1-1/2 cups. Second meal, 1 cup.

Semi-Moist Dog Food

Type: 5.3 oz. pouch of chicken and gravy weight control formula, 136.5 calories/pouch

Sample Diet 1

Dog's weight: 3 pounds

Feeding instructions: Feed a total of 3/4 of a pouch a day. When goal weight is reached, switch to 1 full pouch a day.

Feeding frequency: First meal, 1/2 pouch. Second meal, 1/4 pouch.

Sample Diet 2

Dog's weight: 20 pounds

Feeding instructions: Feed a total of 3-1/4 pouches a day. When goal is reached, increase to 3-1/2 pouches a day.

Feeding frequency: First meal, 2 pouches. Second meal, 1-1/4 pouches.

Sample Diet 3

Dog's weight: 80 pounds

Feeding instructions: Feed a total of 8 pouches a day. When goal weight is reached, increase to 9 pouches.

Feeding frequency: First meal, 5 pouches. Second meal, 3 pouches.

Canned dog food

Type: 14 oz. can of chicken, liver and rice weight control formula, 487 calories

Sample Diet 1

Dog's weight: 10 pounds

Feeding instructions: Feed a total of 1/2 can a day. When goal weight is reached, switch to a maintenance diet of 2/3 can.

Feeding frequency: First meal, 1/4 can. Second meal, 1/4 can.

Sample Diet 2

Dog's Weight: 30 pounds

Feeding instructions: Feed a total of one can per day. When goal weight is reached, switch to maintenance diet of 1-1/4 cans.

Feeding frequency: First meal, 3/4 can. Second meal, 1/4 can.

Just One Fat Minute

Do you really know what one half cup of dry dog food looks like? Go into the kitchen right now (don't tell Fido or Fifi) and measure it out.

Doesn't look like much, does it?

These cases suggest what a diet looks like when you stick strictly to one of the three general types of dog food. Can you—should you—mix different types of foods, spicing up your dog's kibble with semi-moist morsels? Absolutely, if it helps make your dog more comfortable with the diet. Remember, however, to calculate the calories of all the food you give your dog, regardless of type. When in doubt about calories or quantities, check the food package or review the food company's Web site. If you can't locate it, call the company's customer support line. They will be happy to help you establish an accurate calorie count, and even estimate the portion needed to slim down your dog.

HOW OFTEN SHOULD YOU FEED YOUR FAT DOG?

Vets differ about this issue. Dr. Phil Brown, D.V.M., who has consulted with companies such as Newman's Own Organics, is a firm believer that dogs should be fed twice a day, feeling that a dog that eats only once a day is essentially having his system pushed into starvation mode. Others recommend that when a dog is dieting, he needs even more frequent meals, perhaps three or four. Other sources feel that a single feeding time is fine. Perhaps the most important thing is to be accurate about how much your dog is eating, and how often.

Dogs are hardy. The good news about this fantastic, thriving species, is that they really can skip a few meals and snacks, and will, unless there are other health problems, move along just fine. Unlike cats, who cannot go very long without a meal without suffering grave physical consequences, dogs can skip meals with no ill effect. In fact, when a dog is going through a bad tummy problem, you may want him to lay off the kibble for your rug and furniture's sake. Also, all dogs should be fed less when the weather gets warmer (make sure never to stint on water) and during periods of inactivity, such as periods of post-surgery recovery, very cold weather, or recuperation from an illness.

In the spring of 2004, David Muriello trained shelter dogs to help make them more adoptable. This Siberian Husky is being trained to sit while making eye contact.

When feeding a fat dog, here's a mantra to make your own: Nothing In Life Is Free, or NILIF. Dogs had to work for their food in the wild, by stalking it, hunting it, and, yes, sometimes killing it. A lot of hard canine labor went into a single meal.

Certified Pet Dog Trainer David Muriello of New Jersey's "Have A Great Dog" goes pretty far to bring back the hunt into a dog's meal: He recommends taking your dog's bowl of food and tossing it all over the backyard, and make him "look for it." (Don't try this when the yard has been treated with chemicals, of course.) That may sound extreme, but even if you choose something a little less dramatic, it's a healthy reminder that dogs have a long tradition of working for their food, which does two great things—gets your dog some exercise, and, if training is involved, gets you and your dog more intensely bonded.

Could Your Dog Be the Best Weight Loss Coach You Ever Had?

A 2004 study sponsored by Northwestern Memorial Hospital in Illinois and Hill's Pet Nutrition suggests that people and their pets are both more successful in staying with a weight loss program when they exercise together.

Dubbed P-PET (*People and Pets Exercising Together*), the year-long study was made up of three groups of overweight participants: a dog/owner group (36 people and their dogs), a dog-only group (53 dogs), and a people-only group (56 people). The purpose of the study was to compare the efficacy of weight loss programs for dog-only and people-only groups to that of a combined dog/owner weight loss program for both weight loss and weight maintenance.

During the study, dogs were fed a low-fat, nutritionally balanced food, Hill's Prescription Diet® Canine r/d®. In addition, pet owners with dogs in the study were provided with a suggested exercise plan (i.e., 30 minutes of moderate-intensity physical activity at least three days per week) and a regular weigh-in schedule. When the dog's ideal body weight was achieved, the dogs were changed to Hill's Prescription Diet® w/d® food until the 12-month study was completed. People were provided with meal plans and pedometers and were instructed on lifestyle changes to increase exercise and monitor food intake.

The combined dog/owner weight loss program was found to be more effective at maintaining participation than the program in which dogs dieted separately: 80 percent of the dogs in the combined dog/owner group completed the study, versus 68 percent of the dogs-only group. Dogs lost an average of 12 pounds, with a maximum weight loss of 35 pounds. (The average human weight loss was 11 pounds, with a maximum weight loss of 51 pounds.)

The coaching works both ways. While it was clear that it was the owner who had to enroll the dog in the study, once they got going, it was the dog's exercise pattern that helped the owner out. Two-thirds of the increase in physical activity in the combined dog/owner group was obtained by engaging in dog-related activities. In other words, dogs got their owners moving!

Just Five Fat Minutes

The next time you come home from a walk with your dog, play "Hide the Keys." Ask your dog to "take scent," i.e. get a good sniff of your keys, and then go into the next room, close the door, and hide them. Return to your dog, and look bewildered. Lead your dog into the room where you "lost" your keys, and encourage him or her to find them. Depending on the breed, you may want to hide the keys in plain sight, or hide them under a pillow to make the search more challenging. When your dog locates the keys, reward your dog with ONE treat. This will get you and your dog in the habit of adding a little extra exercise at the end of the walk—and of making one treat really have value.

HOW TO CHANGE YOUR DOG'S DIET

Slowly.

Remember the last time you went on a crash diet, eliminating cookies, drinking nothing but clear broth? How did it make you feel? Not great, right? Your dog agrees with you. Don't put him through it, either.

It took time for your dog to gain weight, and it will take time to lose it. Have patience. If you choose to switch your dog from his regular food to a prescription or diet food, make the switch gradually, increasing the ratio of new food to old over the course of 7-10 days. Make a note of the nutritional differences between the food before you start. Pay close attention to how your dog responds to the new food.

And, it has to be said: You'll get good feedback about how your dog's handling his new chow by watching his poop.

Other ways to help ease the diet transition for your dog:

- Feed him in a separate area before you feed yourself. A full-bellied dog is less likely to beg table scraps.
- Divide his meal into three or four portions, so he has something to look forward to.
- Make sure he has fresh water at all times.

HOW DO I STORE MY DOG'S FOOD?

While dogs rarely turn up their noses at any kind of food, you shouldn't depend on them to tell you when something doesn't taste good. You're the one with the discriminating taste buds. With dry kibble, you can choose to leave the food down throughout the day (after you've measured it, of course); discard whatever isn't eaten by day's end. With canned and semi-moist foods, bring the food out twice a day, and return the remainder to the refrigerator 15 minutes after you've set it down.

THE SKINNY ON THIS CHAPTER

- Feed your dieting dog at least twice a day.
- Make your dog work for some of his food, via training or even hunting for his food.
- Consider going on a diet with your dog—research suggests you'll both be more successful.

Exercise with Your Dog

A healthy adult dog needs about the same amount of exercise you do, which is 30 minutes of aerobic exercise, three to four times a week.

But if your dog has become overweight, it's counterproductive to push your dog into a heavy duty exercise program. That would be like putting your dog on a crash diet. This is why it is important, in the early stages of slimming down your dog, to keep careful track of just how much exercise he's getting, and at what intensity. As you and your dog start out, it's better to undertrain than to overtrain.

Begin with a short-term, approachable goal. Just as with humans, you can give your dog exercise in small doses, even when you're inside. The next time you get a phone call, Dr. Jennifer Jellison, D.V.M., of Columbus, Ohio, suggests, pick up your cordless phone and walk from room to room, and signal to your dog that she's supposed to follow you. If your dog is reluctant, pick up a low-fat treat and lure her. It will get both you and your dog in the habit of moving a little while you're in the house. The first level of exercise to target is the minimum, that is, three walks, each 15 minutes in duration. Build from there. What follows in this chapter are both casual and structured ways to get your dog moving.

TRAINING YOUR FAT DOG TO SUCCEED

If you have an overweight dog, and you have never trained him, then the time to start is now. While we won't really know until dogs can talk, it does seem that an awful lot of dogs suffer from a kind of low-grade boredom, as a result of our rushed and modern lifestyle. One book on training bad dogs is even called *The Latchkey Dog*.

One way out of this—and towards a healthier dog—is getting your pudgy pooch some basic training. You owe it to him.

Sometimes a dog's lack of training or unruly personality can contribute to his weight problem. If your dog is aggressive towards people, dogs, or both, you probably exercise him less than he needs, which may have contributed to his extra weight. If your dog has a fear of the outside, you probably exercise him less than he needs, which has contributed to his extra weight. Ironically, your dog's behavior would probably improve if you could exercise him.

These kinds of problems don't resolve by themselves. If your dog is just rambunctious, or suffering from new puppy energy, make sure to invest in a good dog training book, and, ideally, an obedience class.

However, if your dog's behavior makes every walk a misery, seek out a reputable dog trainer. Start with the Association of Pet Dog

Trainers (www.apdt.com), which offers a database of dog trainers. An untrained dog is not just a bad dog—he's probably unhappy, as well. Your dog will thank you, and so will the world at large.

But doesn't dog training involve a lot of treats? And isn't that just what you shouldn't be feeding your overweight dog? Dog trainer Pam Dennison, author of *The Complete Idiot's Guide to Positive Dog Training,* admits that this seems a contradiction. However, she also notes that many dog owners forget that their dogs actually have a wide range of things that make them happy—"life" rewards rather than "food" rewards. Many wound-up dogs will benefit from a fierce game of retrieve, which not only reinforces obedience, but also exercises the heck out of them. She also notes with a laugh that "human beings are boring," in that we tend to rely on the same rewards over and over again when training our pets. She found that the more you vary your dog's rewards, the more alert and responsive the dog tends to be. Before you begin training your dog, pick out four "behavior reinforcers" *besides* a treat that you plan to use to reward him.

TOYS, TOYS, TOYS

No chapter on dog movement could be complete without a discussion of doggie toys. Just as with exercise, pick your dog's toys so they match his personality as well as his physique. There are seemingly millions on the market, but they can be separated into a few categories.

Chew Toys

The best chew toys on the market live long, and bounce like crazy. The gold standard for chew toys is the Kong, a bulbous, bouncy plaything made of nearly indestructible rubber in an infinite number of sizes. There are also a whole host of rubber toys in which you can "hide" treats. The dog either works them out of the toy's crevices, or tips the toy over to release the treats. Especially for a fat dog, this is a good way to emphasize the lesson of Nothing In Life Is Free.

Chew toys like Howell's can protect your dog's dental health.

Chew toys can also be good for your dog's dental health, like the popular Nylabone. If you're trying to improve his teeth, get your dog a chew toy designed to massage your dog's gums.

Regardless of the brand, keep a couple of things in mind: Make sure you buy the right size chew toy for your dog. Too small, and he could swallow it. Too big, and he won't have fun. Replace them if and when your dog chews them down. He'll thank you.

Squeak Toys

Does your dog love things that go squeak? The market has no end of stuffed objects that go squeak. The major challenge for most dog owners is expense; most dogs who love chew toys also love to pull them apart fast. In fact, for many dogs, the real game is "find the squeaker and pull it out." (Remember to take the squeaker away from the dog as soon as it is separated from the toy.) However, if your dog is deeply attached to squeaky toys, the solution is either to seek out the sturdiest of the breed, or to "hide" your dog's squeaky toys so they last longer.

Fetch Toys

Fetch toys help build the bond between you and your dog, while getting him the exercise that he needs. Flying discs and tennis balls are popular choices, with a couple of provisos. Chasing a flying disc can actually cause orthopedic problems in your dog. And you should never leave your dog alone with a tennis ball, which, if the dog opens it with his jaws, could obstruct his airway.

If your dog is a water retriever, look into the Water Kong, which boasts a nice tow rope that helps you throw the toy out far into the water.

Tug of War

To pull or not to pull? The controversy continues about toys that encourage tug-of-war. Especially if you are trying to train your dog, you should limit tug-of-war games to dog vs. dog. You may think you're having a nice game with your dog, but in fact, the dynamics of the game are actually teaching your dog to be dominant, even aggressive. Lots of dogs do play this game without incident, but not all. Don't take the chance.

OUTDOOR ACTIVITIES FOR YOU AND YOUR DOG

With any activity that involves jogging or running, be sure to monitor the bottom of your dog's paws for cuts and tears. If they develop, make sure to moisturize your dog with a dog-friendly lotion or ointment. Meanwhile, if you spend lots of time out in the heat, invest in a portable water bowl or bottle, depending on your access to water.

Jogging

Nothing feels better than running with your dog. In the beginning, make sure to keep the pace on the slow side—a brisk trot is best. If you have a pudgy puppy, wait until he's at least two years old before doing roadwork.

Biking

As with jogging, this is a good way

Even a simple game of catch, like this one with Lucky, can exercise your pooch.

to get everybody's exercise needs met at the same time. Do not bike with your dog's leash in your hands, or wrapped around the handle; it's a recipe for disaster. Look in a pet store or catalog for a device that allows you to keep your hands on the handle bars, and your dog's leash safely attached. As with jogging, this is great play for a grown dog. Puppies' bones are still developing for this challenging exercise.

Swimming

Puppies can begin swimming at the age of three months or so. Much like a dog's love of vegetables, this is a talent that may lie hidden until your dog has the opportunity to explore the water. Hydrotherapist John Larson of the Dog Run swimming pool of New York City says he has never seen a dog come into his pool who doesn't at least learn to tolerate the water. And many learn to love it, to become true "swim-phomaniacs."

There are lots of advantages to swimming for overweight dogs, and few disadvantages. It is truly an exercise for all ages. Because it is a non-weight-bearing exercise, it is a perfect activity for dogs of any size recovering from some kinds of injuries, aging dogs, and dogs suffering from arthritis. And while some dogs are more buoyant than others, they all can learn to float for some amount of time. Dogs with short or docked tails, for instance, such as Boston terriers or Bulldogs, lack the backside ballast to stay on top of the water. Fortunately, there are now such things as "floaty vests" for dogs. Dogs with sensitive eyes can be equipped with dog-shaped goggles known as "Doggles." Nearly every dog, Larson notes, loses weight while swimming, and loses it quickly.

Look for opportunities to help your dog swim. Choose a pond, lake, or pool, never a river. If your dog seems a little skittish about jumping in the water, get yourself some incentive. Invest in a few extra tennis balls, or, our favorite, the Water Kong, a floating version of the typical heavy duty Kong, which includes a bright-colored tow rope, which the dog grabs and tows back to the side of a pool, or into the shallows.

IDENTIFYING YOUR DOG

Whether your dog never goes off-leash, or spends every day bounding in the woods, it only takes a second to lose your dog. An open door, a loose collar, enough confusion, and even the best-trained dog can get lost. Sad to say, despite the movies, dogs don't come home. Therefore, your dog should always carry identification.

At bare minimum, your dog's collar should always have tags that include your current phone number. (Too many people move and forget to update their phone numbers on their dogs' tags.) But lost dogs often lose their collars, too. Other more permanent options include tattooing and microchipping.

With tattooing, your dog is tattooed with a traceable number, such as your driver's license number, or a registry number from the American or Canadian Kennel Clubs. This is a useful tool—if the person who finds your dog a) spots the tattoo and b) has access to the database that contains your dog's trace number.

More recently, owners have begun microchipping their pets. Your vet imbeds a chip in your dog's shoulder with a large needle. The process is brief and relatively inexpensive ($30-$60). The chip is not a locator chip, as some believe (though GPS locator chips for your dogs are on their way.) If your dog is ever lost, anyone with a microchip scanner can "read" your dog's unique number and use it to locate your pooch's home.

You should also register the number on the chip with AKC Companion Animal Recovery (800-252-7894), which, for a $12.50 fee, offers a lifetime, 24-hour, year-round identification service for dogs, cats, horses, lizards, rabbits, birds, and any other companion animal wearing a chip. They also offer a tag with the dog's ID number and the recovery center's number, which could be very helpful if the person who locates your dog doesn't have a microchip scanner handy.

Just Fifteen Fat Minutes

Got a dog who likes to roam? Take a white dog-sized t-shirt and write the following in permanent marker: "Hi, I'm {your dog's name}. I'm on a special diet. Call this number to find out what I can eat." And put this on your dog. This is an actual technique employed by Dr. Martha Gearhart, D.V.M., of Pleasant Valley Animal Hospital in Pleasant Valley, New York.

WEATHERPROOFING YOUR ATHLETIC DOG

In general, dogs are hardy creatures who relish more exercise, not less. However, there are a few important considerations when the weather gets extreme.

Summer

When the weather gets hot and hazy, make sure you have ready access to a water supply for your dog. When your dog overheats, he regulates his temperature by panting. However, he will not be able to tell you when he needs more water, so make sure to have it on hand. Typical signs of an overheated dog include listlessness, swollen tongue, loss of skin elasticity, and dryness of mouth.

Be especially careful if you own a short-nosed (brachycephalic) dog such as a pug, bulldog, Pekingese, and others. Due to the shortness of their nasal passages, they can only spend limited amounts of time in the heat before it affects them.

Winter

Not all dogs are blessed with luxuriant fur coats. Even those that are may need a little extra help. If you are going to exercise your dog in lower temperatures, consider buying a coat or sweater that keeps the dog well-covered. If your dog has to walk sidewalks covered with rock salt or ice, consider getting booties, or a protective paw wax. He will thank you!

FOR SOCIAL DOGS

Dog Park

Is your dog a social dog? One of the ways to get your dog a lot of exercise fast is to find your dog a dog park where he can run off-leash and interact with other dogs who enjoy running around as much as he does.

Dog Day Care

Another option for well-socialized hounds is doggy day care, where you leave your dog for a set number of hours to hang out with, and play with lots of other dogs. If you're leaving your beloved hound at a day care center, establish that it's the kind of place where your dog will have the chance to run around and play—or even swim. For instance, Graceland, a doggy day care center in Hoboken, New Jersey, offers dogs the airy first floor of a loft building to run and play in. It's bright, light, and there's even a very realistic-looking cement tree sitting in the middle of the 6,000 square foot center.

THE SKINNY ON THIS CHAPTER

- Tailor your dog's exercise program to his fitness level AND his personality.
- Jogging or biking with your dog kills two exercise birds with one stone—but make sure only to do this high-impact exercise with a grown dog.
- If your dog is social and reasonably fit, consider enrolling him in an organized activity.
- Toys can extend your dog's exercise by leaps and bounds. If your dog likes to chew and destroy, invest in durable, higher-end toys.

Compete for Most Slim Dog

Choosing an organized activity for your dog to do with you provides both you and the dog with a lot of benefits. When you pick the right sport for your dog, you remind yourself of your dog's ancestral history as an athlete and a hunter. You bond, deeply, with the dog, and strengthen the relationship you had already.

Keep in mind that matching the sport to your dog's gifts is very important. Greyhounds, for instance, were trained to sprint, quickly, over very short distances. They are capable of speeds up to 40 miles an hour, over distances of 9/16th of a mile. While, at the other end of the speed/distance continuum, Alaskan sled dogs can move, for hours, over very long distances—in the Iditarod race for instance, sled dogs pull their handlers over 1,100 miles, during a race that lasts from two to three weeks. It's unlikely an Alaskan sled dog could ever beat a

Greyhound at his own race—just as unlikely that a Greyhound could ever successfully compete in the Iditarod. Relatively speaking, Greyhounds have speed, Alaskan sled dogs have stamina. Ask yourself, where does your dog fit in the mix? And what kind of expectations do you have for your dog? For yourself?

Other breeds exhibit other skills. Until the mid-19th century, it was not uncommon in Europe to see dogs used as draft animals, pulling market carts. Especially popular (and overworked) were breeds such as Samoyeds, Bernese Mountain Dogs, Newfoundlands, and St. Bernard's. Once the use of cart dogs was abolished, owners saw a kinder use for these strong-backed breeds as rescue dogs, particularly in snow or freezing water.

So, when picking an activity, ask yourself: If your dog were a person, what kind of person would he be? What kind of shows would he watch? What kind of sports would he play? It may sound silly, but one of the key tools to really helping your dog lose weight is that it's got to be tailored to the dog. It doesn't have to be suffering and agony. It is about getting healthier, and keeping your dog around longer.

Here is a round-up of games, sports, and competitions you can play with your dog to get that dog moving. This list is far from complete. If you are interested in getting your dog into organized activities, check out the American Kennel Club's web site at www.akc.org, or www.dogpatch.org, for a full round-up of fun events to do with your dog.

AGILITY

In agility trials, dogs race against the clock and take on obstacles that they must go through or jump over. This kind of exercise is for you if you are already in pretty good shape and would like to get into even better shape, and if your dog is only slightly overweight to start. It is also really fun to watch, which is why it seems to show up regularly not just on "Animal Planet," but on talk shows like David Letterman (and not just as part of "Stupid Pet Tricks"), and on Ellen DeGeneres' talk show. (Not only did Ellen lead a dog through an agility course— she also competed. As if she were a dog. The dog's time was better, by the way.)

Rally-O

Relatively new, this sport uses maneuvers similar to competition obedience, while allowing the trainer/handler to speak to the dog through the entire competition, while giving extra cues. The handler leads the dog through a course of signs, and has the dog do the behavior listed on the signs.

EARTHDOG

This competition is for small terriers, such as Jack Russells, who long ago were bred to seek out rodents in the ground. In this modified, no-violence modernization, terriers are released into underground tunnels to seek out caged rodents (who are NOT hunted). Fun for the terrier, maybe not quite so much for the rodents. Still, it is amazing to watch these small dogs do the work that they were originally raised to do.

DANCING

Do you believe that your dog will dance…when pigs fly?

Take heart. Dog dancing, usually known as "freestyle dancing," uses the building blocks of tricks and obedience training, and puts them to music.

You don't have to be John Travolta to dance with your dog, but it helps to have a little basic obedience under you and your dog's belt. Lots of people are already out there, doing it. According to an article in the Fall 2004 BARK magazine, freestyle dog dancing now boasts 50 annual competitions and 10,000 participants. To locate trainers and events near you, check out www.worldcaninefreestyle.org.

But you don't have to join a group or hire a trainer to start dancing with your dog. All you need is a little clear space in your house and some free time. Add some nifty music, your favorite pup, some treats, and a willingness to work with the basic cool moves your dog already has.

Some pets, like Remy, connect mealtime with playtime.

The basic concept of freestyle dancing is the same as any kind of positive conditioning: Catch your dog doing something right, and reward the activity with a treat. Start the music, and practice heeling with your dog. If your dog finds the music too fast or too slow, don't push the dog. Pick a more pup-friendly piece of music.

The core moves of freestyle dancing include:

Spin: With your dog in front of you, lead your dog clockwise in quarter turns until he completes a circle.

Weave: Get your dog to do figure 8's through your legs, using treats as a lure.

Backup: With your dog standing in front of you, and a treat in your hand, advance a step forward. Your dog, magnetized by the treat, will back up. Treat, and repeat.

Hurdle: Make your leg parallel with the floor, and lead the dog over with a treat.

Wildcard: This is any special talent your dog has, from kissing on command to carrying her bowl.

FLYBALL

Did you ever suspect that your dog, along with being an excellent jumper and even more excellent ball retriever, also longs to put those skills to work in a relay team? If so, flyball is your dog's game.

Flyball, which first came to prominence in California in the 1970s, is made up of a course with four hurdles spaced ten feet apart, and a spring-loaded box. The dog leaps the four hurdles, then hits the release on the spring-loaded box, which expels a tennis ball. The dog catches or retrieves the tennis ball, then returns over the four hurdles. He or she does this as a part of a relay team consisting of four dogs in total. While the sport is not for the very overweight or out of shape dog, it embraces all manner of breeds, sizes, and ages of dog. Flyball dogs have competed in front of Michael Jordan, and David Letterman. Because this is a sport that requires both companionship and some equipment, try to locate a trainer or a group to help your aspiring flyballer get started. This will also give you some idea if flyball really is the sport for your dog. If your dog is not fond of other dogs, or is easily distracted, he's probably cut out for something else.

SHEEPHERDING

It's not just for border collies, though they do excel at this "sport." If your dog likes to herd, whether he's a poodle or a pit bull, you can teach your dog how to herd sheep, assuming you have an accessible sheep farm. However, if you'd like to enter your dog in competitions, which are run by the AKC and ASCA (Australian Shepherd Club of America), your canine must be a member of an AKC-approved Herding Group (such as Border Collies, Old English Sheepdogs, and Corgis). For an interesting take on where sheepherding can lead you and your dogs, read dog writer Jon Katz's books about his border collies, who have not only changed his life—they've turned him from a suburban writer living in Montclair, New Jersey into a part-time farmer.

If your dog isn't a natural sheepherder, look into other kinds of activities that are rooted in his breed's original "job," such as field trials, sled dog events, protection dog events, and water dog events.

David Muriello's adopted Border Collie/Shepherd mix, Eli, won his way onto TV performing tricks like "Knockout," where David throws a fake punch and Eli spins and falls over.

THE HELPING PROFESSIONS

Maybe you've got a mellow fat dog on your hands, a dog who listens and obeys, all the time. Maybe a pack of ten screaming children can crawl all over your dog, with no complaint from your dog. When you look up "consistent" in the dictionary, do you think of your dog?

Your fat dog could be a candidate for becoming a therapy dog. Therapy dogs visit hospitals, nursing homes, hospices, to provide a touch of kindness and unconditional love to residents. To become a therapy dog, you and your dog will have to go through a thorough training program. While this training is not necessarily aerobic, it does provide the kind of structure and focus that an underutilized dog needs.

SEARCH, RESCUE...AND CANCER HUNTING

One of the more remarkable things about dogs is their sense of smell, which on a daily basis, they are happy to use to locate, say, a two-day old piece of pizza buried in a snow drift. However, dogs are now being trained to use their noses from anything to identifying cancer...to locating cats.

Some of the newer ways dogs are being trained to use their super-nasal powers include:

- cancer sniffer
- invasive species identifier
- locater of endangered species
- termite locater
- lost cat tracker

With these particular jobs, your dog either had to enroll (there is actually a cat tracking school run by a pet detective) or be recruited (physicians in Britain and the U.S. are now training dogs to identify cancer in human patients, with some early success). However, without sending your dog across country, consider exploring just how powerful your dog's sense of smell is by encouraging him to "find" things you hide in the house or in the yard. You'll be surprised at how energized this makes the average dog.

THE SKINNY ON THIS CHAPTER

- Match your dog's personality and body type to a healthy activity. Social dogs need social games; solitary dogs may be happiest just running with you.
- Consider joining an organized group to up your dog's exercise.
- Use every opportunity to use your dog's senses to exercise him, from hiding his favorite toy to taking him on a hunt for your keys.

Help Your Older Dog Adjust

The good news about your dog is, thanks to advances in veterinary medicine, he has an excellent chance of living longer. A current estimate puts the number of dogs 10 years and older at 7.3 million. The average dog now lives 13 years; some dogs are now living into their 20s.

Now, how does he live fitter?

Because geriatric dogs are generally less active, they require up to 30% fewer calories than younger dogs. But that doesn't mean they need less activity—just different types of activity. And while it does mean fewer calories, it also means an even sharper focus on nutrition, particularly, it seems, on antioxidants.

The key to getting your older overweight dog healthy and slim is to go slow and steady.

Slow. If he is overweight, your older dog should lose no more than 1.5% of his body weight per week. Any more, and you will be putting too much stress on his body. You may want to choose a senior dog food, but if your dog is happy with his current food, don't feel the need to change unless your vet recommends it. (As always, make sure that your dog has a clean bill of health; older dogs sometimes have underlying physical problems that do require a special diet.) An older dog requires 25 to 30 calories per pound of body weight. Focus on making sure your dog is getting the right blend of vitamins, minerals, and antioxidants. As listed below; there's even some research that suggests the right blend of antioxidants will boost your dog's smarts.

Steady. As your dog ages, encourage him to engage in low-impact or no-impact exercise in short, consistent sessions. You may have spent your dog's early years on five-mile runs; now is the time to switch to walks, strolls, and, especially, swimming.

THE SKINNY ON YOUR OLD DOG'S AGING PROCESS

The arrival of senior years varies wildly from breed to breed. Some large working dogs arrive at midlife at their fifth birthday, while other breeds (and mixed breeds) show no sign of aging until they turn at least eight. If you have a purebred dog, you probably have a reasonable benchmark of when to start thinking of your pet as an older dog—but keep in mind both temperament and health history may play equally big role in your dog's "real age." (For more on how to measure your dog's "real age," try taking an online test at **www.dogage.com**.)

During the first couple of years of life, dogs generally age at the same rate. When your puppy turns one, he is the equivalent of a 16-year-old physically and mentally. At age two, your dog resembles a fit 24-year-old. Then, after that, on average, your dog ages about five dog years for every human year.

But even with this rule of thumb, there are great variations. Giant breeds generally age much faster than smaller breeds; mixed breeds are praised for their "hybrid vigor" and hardiness—but they can also take on many of the vulnerabilities of their original breeds.

Dogs with large snouts seem to live longer than their flatter-faced brothers and sisters; small (but not tiny) live longer than larger. Regardless of the size or snout of your dog, observe this rule of thumb: Starting between the ages of six and eight, your older dog should have a complete physical every year, even if he has never, ever been ill. This exam gives your vet a baseline of good health to work from. And you owe it to your dog. The exam should include a physical, complete blood count, blood chemistries, urinanalysis, and parasite examination. His teeth should also be checked and cleaned; in some cases, some dogs will need more frequent dental checkups. At home, if you haven't been brushing your dog's teeth, it's time to begin.

WHAT IS HAPPENING TO YOUR OLD DOG?

Your dog's body slows down as it ages, and some of his senses grow less sharp. Typically, you will see these kinds of changes:

Vision and hearing change. Many dogs do experience a diminishment of hearing and sight, from minor to major, but your dog's beacon in the world is his ultra strong sense of smell, which allows him to maneuver in the world even if he doesn't hear or see well. Still, if you know that your dog no longer hears or sees as well as he used to, make sure that you always keep him leashed while on your walks.

Incontinence. It's an unhappy fact of some older dogs' lives. It's important to take your dog to the vet when he seems to be having more accidents than he used to, to make sure that there isn't some physical problem causing the dog's bathroom problems. Fortunately, there are options to take care of your dog, including doggie diapers, a very regulated bathroom schedule, and changes in diet. **Do not reduce your dog's water intake to "fix" the problem**—this can cause kidney problems.

Lumps. Many dogs, as they age, develop benign fatty tumors. They typically are round, soft, and easy to find—and no big deal. But to make sure of it, report them to the vet as soon as you find them.

Stiffness. Is it muscle soreness or is it arthritis? Your vet can help you figure it out. If it's the normal kind of stiffness that lots of creatures, including older humans, go through in the morning you might resolve that issue by making simple changes—changing your dog's bedding so that it provides more support, adapting the kind of play you do with your dog, and, very importantly, lessening the intensity, but **increasing** the frequency of your dog's exercise session. Think low-stress, but frequent bursts of exercise.

If it is arthritis, treatment can include weight loss, non-impact exercise such as swimming, anti-arthritis drugs such as Rimadyl, and nutraceuticals such as glucosamine and chondroitin.

Cancer. Sadly, the majority of dogs who contract cancer are middle-aged and older. However, just as with human medicine, there have been some remarkable advances in treating cancer in dogs, and the survival rate is increasing. When your dog is undergoing cancer treatment, discuss with your vet just what kind of modifications you need to make in your dog's eating and exercise patterns.

Perception and cognition. Simply put, as your dog ages, your dog's brain doesn't fire up as quickly as it used to, and it becomes less flexible. Research suggests that there are ways around this process. Just as you may be doing crossword puzzles to keep your brain nimble, your older dog needs physical and mental challenges to keep his brain healthy and flexible. A recent University of Toronto study cited by Stanley Coren in his book *How Dogs Think* suggests that while it may not solve every dog's problems, some older dogs can really benefit from a "brain-rich" diet and a more stimulating environment.

TEACHING OLD DOGS NEW TRICKS THROUGH DIET AND PLAY

Can extra servings of carrots and extra games of "hide the treat" make your aging dog smarter? Some old beagles would tell you, yes. Researchers at the University of Toronto have completed a study that suggested that certain kinds of food could make your old dogs smarter, especially if you challenge their intelligence at the same time. During a two-year study, the team fed a group of 24 old beagles (ages 8 to 11) a diet rich in antioxidants, and a second set of 24 a standard balanced diet.

Within these two groups, exactly half of each group received "cognitive enrichment," such as being challenged to find hidden food or distinguish between a black box and a white box, five to six days a week.

Hanz, an elderly pudgy pooch, has just begun his diet.

When the entire group of 48 beagles were retested at the end of a year, the group that scored the highest on mental ability tests were the dogs on the antioxidant-rich diets who were also cognitively enriched. (The dogs who were only fed the diet, or only performed "mental agility" also improved—but not as much as the group who got the double dose of antioxidant-rich food and challenging play.)

How do you replicate this effect with your dog in your own house? You could choose to feed your dog the same food the beagles received (it is now available as a prescription diet for dogs through Hill's Pet Nutrition). But if you prefer to customize your dog's diet, you could pick from the following to add antioxidants, vitamin E, beta-carotene and other carotenoids, and selenium, all elements of the "smart old dog" diet, to your dog's existing food. The sources for these nutrients include fruits, vegetables, whole grains, poultry, fish, meat, and eggs.

To increase your older dog's intake of vitamin C, feed your dog citrus fruits, green peppers, broccoli, strawberries, raw cabbage, potato, and steamed or parboiled green leafy vegetables.

To give your dog high doses of Vitamin E, feed your dog wheat germ, nuts, seeds, whole grains, steamed or parboiled green leafy vegetables, vegetable oil, and fish liver oil.

To provide your dog with beta-carotene and carotenoids, try carrots, squash, broccoli, sweet potatoes, tomatoes, kale, collard greens, cantaloupe, peaches, and apricots.

To add selenium to your dog's diet, try fish, shellfish, red meat, grains, eggs, and chicken.

The second part of the "diet" is activity, the more challenging the better. When was the last time you did teach your old dog a new trick? Start today.

HOW TO KEEP YOUR DOG MOVING THROUGH HIS SENIOR YEARS

1. Pay close attention. Don't expect your old dog to tell you that he's sore by moaning or whimpering; while it's pretty clear that dogs suffer pain in the way humans do, they are typically far more stoic than humans are. Back in the day when dogs were still wolves, the worst possible thing a wounded wolf could do would be to whimper; it would have made him a target for other predators. Dogs retain some of that breeding. As a responsible owner, keep track of just how easily your dog moves. Look, for example, at how comfortable he is going up and down steps. Does he hesitate when jumping? When your dog begins to walk more stiffly or more slowly, stay calm, and don't decide to eliminate exercise altogether.

2. Become a genuine student of who your dog is now. Don't push, but don't let him slack off, either. Even if he isn't overweight, keep a dog log for two or three days to mark just what he likes to eat, and how he likes to move. Are there games your dog can play better than when he was younger? For instance, while your dog's eyes and ears may be less sharp, his

When the Owner Needs Rehab

What if you're the one who suffers the injury? It isn't easy, but it can be done. Marathon runner Penny Wagner has three four-legged running partners: Fast Eddie, Emma Biaggio, and Boomer Sabastiano, all Jack Russell Terriers. When Penny is in training, she and her dogs typically run six or seven miles a day. But in September of 2004, Penny was hit by a car. In the aftermath, she suffered a broken ankle that required surgery—and had to stop running completely for three months while she went through physical rehabilitation.

During Penny's rehabilitation, the only exercise the dogs got were Penny's morning and evening walks. Penny, an experienced athlete, realized that she wasn't the only one who had to adapt to her injury. "I first noticed that my oldest {dog} Fast Eddie, had a weight problem when I felt his fur," Penny says. "I give my dogs massages each day and know this is a good way to also check for tumors. I felt his skin and immediately grabbed a handful of fat that was not there before my accident." All of the dogs, she noted, moved more slowly and were less likely to jump and more likely to be asked to be picked up.

So Pam took action. She changed their food from a high-intensity active dog mix to a food for less-active dogs. She monitored how much she fed them, and cut way back on treats. The result is that after almost two months of their modified diet, the dogs are almost at their normal weights.

It hasn't always been easy. The dogs complained about their lack of treats, and Penny has cut the word "run" out of her vocabulary until they actually can go out on the road again. But Penny credits her dogs with keeping her strong while she recovered and they adapted to their modified lifestyle. "I learned patience from them because they are a very stubborn breed and usually get what they go after, and hope because I knew it was a matter of time before we could all be athletically conditioned athletes as before this temporary setback." As of this writing, she's about to start back running, and so are her dogs.

sense of smell may be just as good, perhaps even heightened. Instead of having him chase a ball, why not consider hiding your keys or a favorite toy and leading your dog on a vigorous search through the house? When roughhousing, think gentle. When you are playing catch or tug of war, try to avoid leaping, twisting, or hard landings.

3. Just as with humans, older dogs need warm-up and cooldown periods to bookend their exercise. Try to begin and end your play sessions with a nice, ambling walk.

    Remember, with older dogs, the key is short, frequent bouts of moderate exercise.

4. Keep him warm and comfortable. Older dogs have a tougher time maintaining their body temperature. Thanks to the explosion of pet supply boutiques, you can find a fashionable coat to fit anything from a teacup breed to a giant. But it isn't always necessary to buy a thing. You may have an old sweater that, with a few minor adjustments, will look just fantastic on Rex or Trixie. Still others choose to knit their own sweaters. Pay particular attention to your dog's body heat issues if he is short-haired, slender, or the member of a toy breed. Don't make his body work too hard in the outside world, especially when it's cold.

    To make your dog's sleep time more comfortable, you may want to invest in an orthopedic bed. Choose a bed that is easy for your dog to get in and out of, but provides your pal with adequate support.

5. If your dog is genuinely suffering from mobility issues, get

help now. Invest in ramps, support leashes, and when necessary, dog carts (sometimes known as doggie wheelchairs). Many aging dogs experience weakness in the back legs, or spinal problems; thanks to a growing group of companies that manufacture assistive devices for pets, you can probably find a product that will help your dog move more, and move happily. The Internet offers many resources, from e-mail lists to Web sites, to aid the owners of dogs with permanent disabilities. If the movement issue is more temporary, ask your vet about physical therapy, hydrotherapy, and acupuncture, all of which can add happy, mobile time to your dog's life.

DOGS WITH SPECIAL NEEDS

While many dogs may suffer impairments either because of age, accident, or illness, it rarely affects their athletic fire. And just as with their owners, the improvements in treatment make it possible for dogs to recover more quickly, and return to a greater range of motion than ever before.

Thanks to the big sea change in the way people view their pets, the business and the medicine of caring for disabled pets has changed radically. Think of how many episodes of television shows about emergency vets feature dogs who have run afoul of a car, or who accidentally tangle themselves in something, leading to a bone fracture. The great news is this rarely means the end of the road for the dog. But it does nearly always means a period of rest and rehab for your dog. And that's when the pounds come on very easily.

After your dog's injury is stabilized, have a genuine discussion with your vet about how long it will take for your dog to recuperate. Generally, with a sprain or a fracture, this means cutting down on a dog's walks, runs, and training sessions by a substantial amount for a long period of time. Which means he will be burning fewer calories for a while. While it's tempting to spoil your dog as he recuperates, this is absolutely the last thing you want to do. Modify your dog's diet and change his food immediately. And, if at all possible, look for alternate forms of exercise and, when necessary, rehabilitation. Here are three major ways to help your dog recover.

Physical Therapy

Some of the canine conditions that benefit from physical therapy include hip dysplasia, arthritis, sprains, tendonitis, cruciate ligament tears, disc disease, paralysis, and de-innervated muscles. It can also help obese or out-of-shape dogs, as well as dogs who have recently undergone surgery. A dog who goes through physical therapy typically can experience reduced pain and discomfort, increased strength and endurance, decreased muscle tightness and spasms, increased range of motion of joints, more rapid surgical recovery, and reduced scar tissue. If your current vet doesn't provide it, ask for a referral.

Hydrotherapy

While your dog is on the mend, do everything you can to keep him well-exercised and supple. With few exceptions, one of the best exercises out there for a temporarily disabled dog is hydrotherapy, whether in the form of physical therapy, guided swimming, or a free swim.

At the Dog Run in New York, hydrotherapist John Larson works with all ages and all sizes of dogs, many of whom have temporary or permanent disabilities. Almost all show some improvement. Larson reports that the oldest dog he's worked with was 20 years old—and that dog swam for a year and half.

The great thing about hydrotherapy is that it offers a disabled dog two major benefits: Exercise that is non-weight-bearing, and a range of stretch that's impossible when the dog is planted on all four feet on the ground.

Puppies under the age of three months shouldn't swim because they aren't developed enough yet. Dogs with stitches, open wounds, or suffering from major tumors should not undergo hydrotherapy, says Larson. Other than that, Larson asserts, he hasn't met a dog who hasn't been able to at least tolerate swimming, and most end up loving it. And nearly every dog who swims regularly gets calmer, leaner, and thinner.

Acupuncture

Acupuncture has reached the medical mainstream for humans, and it's now becoming more standard for veterinary practices to offer it. Acupuncture, invented in China approximately 3,500 years ago, consists of inserting small needles under the skin to aid in various healing processes. Eastern medicine theorizes that, among other things, the needles move the energy. Western medicine theorizes that the needles stimulate production of endorphins, one of the body's natural painkillers. Whatever the theory, acupuncture appears to increase function and mobility in disabled dogs, and is used in treatments for a wide range of problems, from slipped discs to muscle spasms to arthritis. In addition to helping disabled animals regain function, Dr. Martha Gearhart, D.V.M., of Pleasant Valley Hospital, who is certified by the International Veterinary Acupuncture Society (IVAS), feels that her acupuncture training has improved her day-to-day diagnostic skills as a vet. More and more vets offer this as a service. To locate a vet in your area, check out the American Holistic Veterinary Medical Association Director (www.ahvma.org).

THE SKINNY ON THIS CHAPTER

- Thanks to modern veterinary medicine, a record number of dogs are surviving into what use to be considered "old age."
- With aging, dogs do slow down both physically and mentally, but that is all the more reason to watch their diet and exercise.
- If your aging dog is overweight, help him lose the weight slowly. An aging dog should lose no more than 1.5% of his body weight per week.
- An antioxidant-rich diet and brain challenging exercise may actually improve your dog's mental and physical functions.
- Acupuncture, massage, physical therapy, selective use of antioxidants, and water therapy can all contribute to increasing your dog's mobility and ability to exercise.
- Dogs with disabilities due to aging, illness, or injury, can still exercise. Remember to modify their diets to reflect their changed activity levels.

Deal with a Multi-Pet Household

Dr. Jennifer Jellison is a respected vet and researcher with a thriving practice, a bubbly personality, a groundbreaking study on pets and people exercising together (it's all good news)…and an overweight dog.

Dr. Jellison's dog is a retired service dog, who, in the course of training, learned how to open the refrigerator for his owner. Now, while there's no practical reason to do it, Dr. Jellison's dog just keeps on going to the refrigerator. And that's not all, the dog is aces at swiping the cat's food.

Dr. Jellison loves all of her pets, and she figures that having a chubby dog teaches her the kind of empathy that case studies don't provide. But there are good ways and bad ways to negotiate the multi–pet household, and, as with much of this book, it begins with assessment.

If you have the luxury of thinking about what kind of pet you want to add to your household, take the time to do it before the pet arrives. To a certain degree, we've all been conned by the many cartoons and heartwarming movies that suggest that most animals can learn to live in harmony. Rare is the movie or story where the more complicated truth is told, that when it comes to adding a dog or cat to a one-dog family, it's very important to negotiate territory first.

If you believe that another pet will "inspire" your dog to greater heights of exercise and/or good behavior, pause for a moment. When was the last time you had a roommate forcibly introduced to your home? How inspirational was that?

WHEN DOG MEETS DOG

There are all kinds of ways your one-dog kingdom can become a two–dog house. Maybe you've got an older dog, and you think he'd benefit from a younger companion. Maybe you go to a pet adoption fare, and some new furry face just steals your heart. Maybe you take on another dog because a friend has to move to a new place, where dogs aren't welcome.

If you have the opportunity to think about it before adding another dog to the mix, do. Ask yourself the following questions about The Dog Who's Already There:

Is my dog a dog-friendly dog?

Does your dog play well with other dogs? Many dogs don't, and if you've had your dog for any length of time, you know the answer.

Getting even a mildly dog-aggressive dog to behave well on the street is a lot of work. Imagine how much more difficult it would be when the new dog moves into your old dog's space. Don't try it, unless forced to by an emergency. If forced to by an emergency, contact a trainer or animal behaviorist immediately.

Here are the basics when dog meets dog:

- They should first meet on neutral territory—on the street, in a park, or at another person's house.
- Before meeting, they should both be spayed or neutered. (Intact males are notorious for starting fights.)
- Assume jockeying for position will occur, and plan, in advance, how you could remove either or both dogs from the area.
- Train them both at the same time, especially in dominance-defeating behaviors such as "Down-Stay." Two dogs lying in a protracted down cannot get themselves into trouble.
- If there is a substantial age and/or ability difference between the dogs, train the more peppy one to stay while the other one enjoys some solo play. Sometimes the older dog gets the short end of the exercise stick.
- In a multidog household, big, meaty bones are not a good idea. Dogs generally don't know how to share such a tasty treat, and fights can break out.

WHEN DOG MEETS CAT

If you are determined to have two species live in harmony, consider this:

- Always leash your dog when first introducing him to a cat.
- Be prepared to have your cat freak out, and make sure that you

Be prepared for a showdown, like this one between Stinky and Loki, when you introduce a new pet into the house.

can quickly remove the dog from his presence. Allow your cat to retreat to his own space or crate.

- Once the cat is in your house, don't push it. Let the cat pick how much time he wants to spend with a dog.
- On both sides, enthusiastically reward good behavior around the other creature. Load these interactions with treats, so that each pet begins to associate the other with tasty food.
- Especially in a dieting household, position each creature's food so the other can't get at it. Put the cat's bowl out of dog's reach. And consider hand feeding your dog, or closely monitoring his meal times.

- Remember to train your dog well enough to put him in a "Down-Stay." Your cat will thank you.
- If your dog likes to eat gross things, he may invade your cat's litter box, which is filled with protein-rich poop. Consider investing in a covered litter box.

Will your second animal prove to be the fitness coach you hope for? Only time and personality will tell. There's no question that adding a second pet enriches your dog's environment. It's up to you to make sure it stays fun.

Careful assessment and a sensible period of adjustment helps make it fun. Janine Adams' cat Joe was a rescue, and she knew right off that Joe was dog-friendly—because Joe's foster family had seen Joe sleeping with the household dogs! Pip, Janine's cat-crazy standard poodle, and Janine's first pet, clearly loved cats—he actually likes to lick them affectionately. Still, during Joe the cat's first few days in his new house, Joe stayed in a guest room, under a bed, with all interaction between Joe and Pip carefully supervised. In Janine's words, "Joe hung out under the bed for the first few days, but he would come out for licks from Pip." As the years have gone by, Pip no longer licks Joe. Joe and Pip now spend quality time snuggling together on the couch—not exactly aerobic.

However, Joe's fitness coach personality emerged when Janine added Kirby, another poodle, who loves chasing and playing with Joe, who returns the favor. And at mealtime? All three pets eat peacefully together, under the watchful eye of their owner.

What about other kinds of animals? Kate Reilly's original pet

Milo, a Jack Russell, enjoys hanging out with his new cat pal Abel.

household consisted of two guinea pigs who lived in a large Rubbermaid tub on the floor—the better for her kids to access the guinea pigs. When Kate added a retriever/ setter mix with a very high prey drive, a lot of things had to change. When it was clear that the dog thought that the guinea pigs were for pouncing on, Kate moved the guinea pigs off the floor, and began an intensive round of obedience training with the dog and the guinea pigs. This includes on-leash training where the dog learned to sniff the guinea pigs gently, crating the dog in the same room as the guinea pigs, and creating a "guinea pigs only" room, which the dog is not allow to enter. Kate's household is a success. Does she think it made her dog thinner? No. But she thinks the intensive training has made him a better dog.

THE SKINNY ON THIS CHAPTER

- Adding a second pet to your household should be a deliberate process.
- Make sure the first dog is flexible enough to accept a second pet.
- Ramp up any training you're doing to encourage good behavior.
- Make sure each pet has his own separate turf; consider separate meal times and feeding areas.

Maintain Your Dog's Weight Loss

If you've gotten this far, congratulations! It's possible—even likely—that your dog has begun to slim down as a result of your efforts. The key is to be vigilant. Just as with humans, maintaining your dog at a healthy weight is a lifetime job.

So if you find your dog's weight creeping up, it's time to review this book's basics:

1. Start with a healthy baseline. Get your dog checked out by a vet to rule out any medically related causes for his extra weight.

2. Depending on his age, pick a weight loss goal of 1-2% per week. Remember that this will mean that victory comes in ounces!

3. Take out, or buy, measuring cups for your dog's food—and use them.

4. For at least three days, keep a written record of what your dog eats and drinks. Don't forget treats.

5. Gradually increase the amount of exercise for your dog.

6. Explore new forms of exercise for your dog, from swimming to flyball. Look for a sport or activity, perhaps even competition, that matches your dog's breed and/or personality.

7. Make your dog's weight loss program a family affair. Don't assume that just because you're not feeding your dog any treats, your spouse or children are sticking to the rules.

8. Keep your older dog moving through his senior years. If he has mobility issues, investigate ramps, support leashes, and other equipment to help him stay active.

9. Don't assume a second pet will automatically make your dog more active; be prepared for a period of adjustment.

10. Congratulate yourself for keeping your dog fit and thin. You've added months, perhaps years to his life.

Just Ten Fat Minutes

For the dog owner in a rush, here are ten tips in under ten minutes to minimize your canine companion and maximize his fun with you.

1.　The next time you're in a grocery or specialty foods store, buy a little of four different kinds of vegetables—carrots, green beans, cherry tomatoes, green peppers—for your dog. Then surprise him.

2.　If your dog is on a diet, weigh him at least once a week.

3.　If your dog has reached his senior years, schedule a vet checkup that includes a dental cleaning.

4.　Create or review your "dog log."

5.　Buy your dog a new dog toy.

6.　Locate the nearest dog park or agility course in your area.

7.　Call your dog's best friend and set up a play date.

8.　Pick one new thing to teach your dog. Pamela Dennison's *Positive Dog Training* offers a number of easy-to-learn training methods.

9.　Massage your dog. You don't have to be an expert at it. Give him a nice five minute rubdown. Meanwhile, you can check for weight gain or loss, as well as lumps.

10.　Make your walk just a minute longer today. Next week, make it two minutes.

Resources

ADDITIONAL INFORMATION

www.MyFatDogBook.com

For more diet and exercise tips, visit the official *My Fat Dog* Web site. You can also contact the author at Martha@myfatdogbook.com.

MEDICAL INFORMATION AND PET INSURANCE

www.petinsurance.com

The oldest and largest pet insurance company in the United States, founded in 1990 by a vet.

www.peteducation.com

The medical information Web site and online newsletter of the Doctors Foster and Smith catalog; includes instructional videos and real medical cases from vets.

www.pedigree.com

Offers online weight coaching in the form of advice and newsletters to owners of pudgy pooches.

The Internet Animal Hospital

www.thepetcenter.com

This dog and cat health care site is written and maintained by practicing veterinarians. You can view x-rays of actual cases, see real surgery photos, learn about pet foods and nutrition, and more.

PET SUPPLIES AND TOYS

www.jbpet.com

JB Wholesale Pet Supplies, owned by dog fanciers (including one who has bred more than 188 AKC champions), offers over 5,000 items, including beds, grooming products, clothing, leashes, supplements, dental, ear and eye care, and of course toys.

www.doggles.com

Protective eyewear for active dogs that blocks 100 percent of the UV rays, as well as protecting dogs from windblown grit (or excessive chlorine, if they're in the pool).

www.cleanrun.com

This Web site of "the only publisher in the world dedicated exclusively to the needs of the dog agility community" also offers lots of resources on toys, training (clicker and dog agility), treats, flyball, and obedience training.

SPORTS AND TRAINING

Association of Pet Dog Trainers

www.apdt.com

This 5000-member, world-wide organization, founded by respected vet Dr. Ian Dunbar, offers a guide on how to pick a trainer for your dog, and a trainer directory.

National Association of Dog Obedience Instructors

www.nadoi.org

This 40-year-old organization offers resources both for the professional dog trainer and the curious dog owner. All trainers listed on their directory must have worked for five years in the field with a minimum of 100 dogs.

www.clickertraining.com

The Web home of Karen Pryor, one of the premier trainers and scholars of clicker training.

www.musicaldogsport.org

Includes an online workshop section detailing both the philosophy and basic moves of the canine freestyle.

www.worldcaninefreestyle.org

The Web site of a global non-profit canine musical freestyle group, whose founder hopes to someday see the sport in the Olympics. Includes events and workshop schedules, a list of clubs, and a product catalog.

www.caninewatersports.com

Canine Water Sports offers all dogs who love water and the people who love them a wide variety of classes and events, ranging from team swim to water retrieval to search and rescue.

www.flyball.org
The website of the North American Flyball Association.

SPECIAL NEEDS DOGS

www.petswithdisabilities.org
An inspirational Web site recently featured in Dog Fancy and the Today show. Created by the owners of two disabled dogs (Duke and Misty) and Josh a disabled dog-loving cat, this site offers a guide to adopting a diabled pet, stories of thriving disabled pets, as well as an adoption board. Duke and Misty are available for lectures!

www.handicappedpets.com
Products, services, and support for elderly, disabled, and handicapped pets. Includes reviews of products, and an active, informative bulletin board.

www.deltasociety.org
A wealth of information on animal-assisted therapy.

AND JUST FOR FUN

www.dogster.com
Based on the "Friendster" model, a great place to post pictures of your dog, brag about your dog's athletic ability and weight loss, and connect with other dogs and dog owners all over the world. Your dog (and you) can even keep an online diary of your diet success.

Recommended Reading

Adams, Janine. *You Bake 'Em Dog Biscuits*. Running Press, 2004.

Coren, Stanley. *How Dogs Think*. Free Press, 2004.

Dennison, Pamela. *Positive Dog Training*. Alpha, 2003.

Donaldson, Jean. *Culture Clash*. James and Kenneth, 1997.

Giffin, James M. and Liisa D. Carlson. *Dog Owner's Home Veterinary Handbook*. Hungry Minds, 2000.

McCullough, Susan. *Senior Dogs for Dummies*. Wiley, 2004.

Pitcairn, Richard H., and Susan Hubble Pitcairn. *Dr. Pitcairn's Complete Guide to Natural Health for Dogs and Cat*. Rodale, 1995.

Pryor, Karen. *Don't Shoot the Dog*. Bantam, 1999.

Shojai, Amy. *PETiquette: Solving Behavior Problems in Your Multi-Pet Household*. M. Evans & Co., 2005.

Spadafori, Gina. *Dogs for Dummies*. Wiley, 2000.

Spector, Morgan. *Clicker Training for Obedience*. Sunshine, 1999.

Szabo, Julia. *Animal House Style*. Bulfinch, 2001.

Photo Credits

Special thanks to our photographers: